A PILGRIM'S GUIDE TO THE

Camino Inglés

Ferrol & Coruña – Santiago

The English Way also known as the Celtic Camino

T0006538

CAMINO GUIDES.COM

A Practical & Mystical Manual
for the Modern-day Pilgrim

John Brierley

First edition published in 2016 as a combined edition with Camino Finisterre.

ISBN: 978-1-912216-36-9

British Library Cataloguing-in-Publication Data.
A catalogue record for this book is available from the British Library.

Printed in Czechia.

Published by

CAMINO GUIDES
An imprint of Kaminn Media Ltd
272 Bath Street,
Glasgow, G2 4JR

Tel: +44 (0)141 354 1758
Fax: +44 (0)141 354 1759
Email: info@caminoguides.com
www.caminoguides.com

Marina de Ferrol

CONTENTS:

Welcome to the Camino Inglés, *the Celtic Camino.* Recent years have seen a surge in the popularity of this ancient route that follows the rugged *rías* of northern Galicia to Santiago de Compostela. The rise in pilgrim numbers has encouraged significant investment in this route, which is now well waymarked and supported by an ample, and ever growing, network of pilgrim facilities. These developments mean navigating your way along the Camino Inglés is easier than ever. That said, an accurate map and guidebook is useful to help you plan your itinerary and excursions and to put you back on the path when your mind wanders and your feet follow!

A pilgrimage takes place upon two paths, the *outer* path on which our feet tread and the *inner* path of soul. In the following pages we have endeavoured to find a balance between the two by paying equal respect to both. That is why these guides are subtitled *a practical **and** mystical manual for the modern-day pilgrim.* Our wish is that we might find a place to lay our weary head at the end of the day but also, and crucially, that we might feel supported and encouraged to dive into the mysteries of our individual souls awakening.

Pilgrimage offers us an opportunity to slow down and allow some spaciousness into our lives. It encourages us to ask the perennial question, Who am I? And crucially, it provides time for answers to be understood. We may find that Santiago is not the end of the way but the beginning of something entirely new. Whichever route we take, our ultimate destination is assured. The only choice we have is how long it takes us to arrive. *Buen camino – John.*

ABOUT THE AUTHOR: *John Brierley 1948–2023.*
For a quarter of a century John Brierley was inspired by the Caminos de Santiago. He fervently believed in their inherent power to foster positive change, in our individual lives and in the world through changing the way we view our place in it. These guides are the product of

John in Santiago. Portrait by Patti Silva

a calling he felt to encourage pilgrims to embark on both an *outer* journey, as well as to consider their steps along an *inner* journey. The following pages are filled with his enthusiasm and profound belief in the importance of both. They also contain clear and concise information on where to find a cup of coffee in the morning, a ritual as important to him as prayer.

In 2023 John took his final steps on this earthly pilgrimage, but his passion, wisdom and energy live on in the works he left behind. While the practical information in these guides continues to be updated by his daughter, the message is, and will always remain his. To make each step a prayer, to open our hearts with loving kindness and always to keep exploring, both the *outer* world around us and our own *inner* landscape.

NOTES TO THIS EDITION: When the first edition of this guide was printed the number of pilgrims on this route was minimal and arguably so were facilities. Since that time pilgrim numbers have more than doubled and a number of new albergues, both private and Xunta, have opened.

It is not difficult to understand why interest and excitement in the Camino Inglés has continued to grow, with its dramatic coastal location and the white sandy beaches that connect the sea with the green landscape inland. The magic of this route also lies in the mystery of its Celtic connections and the long history of seafaring pilgrims who journeyed to this corner of the world against all odds. There is something special in beginning a pilgrimage with the sea at your back and walking all the way to the spires of Santiago. This is appealing in and of itself but also because one can do so in a relatively short space of time.

Within the context of rising cost of living and growing financial burdens, both income and free time can become squeezed meaning "time out" is an increasingly hard won prize. Yet in these circumstances I would argue that the space provided by pilgrimage is needed more than ever. Against this backdrop the longer routes to Santiago may seem unattainable, but the idea of walking only a part of a route can leave us feeling we have missed out. This is not so with the Camino Inglés. It is not only the length and geographic position that make this route so accessible, the recent investment in facilities and waymarking means that everyone from seasoned veterans to those on their first pilgrimage can find what they need on these paths.

We continue to inhabit a world where change seems to be the only constant. However, we trust that, despite the inevitability of change, the information here will be more than ample to guide you gracefully to Santiago. Along the way you will meet fellow wanderers and the locals who call this land home. But above all you may meet your Self, and that may make all the difference. So journey well. *Buen Camino*.

OVERVIEW CAMINO INGLÉS *The English Way... also known as the Celtic Camino.* Classically Galician, this route takes us from coastal estuaries *rías* through the forests and rolling hills of this rugged corner of Green Spain *España Verde.* This ancient way has a long and varied history as well as a dramatic and beautiful coastal itinerary, so it is not surprising to see that it is fast growing in popularity.

The English Way earned its name due to the large number of pilgrims from north-western Europe, notably England and Ireland, who travelled by sea to the Spanish ports of A Coruña and Ferrol before continuing their pilgrimage on foot to Santiago. Records dating back to the 11th Century tell of pilgrims using these nautical routes and setting sail from English and Irish ports on trade ships bound for the Western coast of Spain. However, the journey by sea was dangerous, so others chose to lengthen the land passage by taking the shorter channel crossing to France, before continuing their journey by foot along one of the land routes, in particular the *Via Turonensis* via Tours.

In the 14th & 15th century the Hundred Years War between England and France made the journey overland more dangerous, leading pilgrims to take once again the longer nautical route direct to Galicia. The Camino Inglés became so popular during this period that the English crown began to issue special licences to vessels carrying pilgrims. Bristol, Portsmouth & Dartmouth were the most popular starting points, with records showing numerous ships named after Saint James. Ships also sailed from several ports in Ireland, with St. James Gate in Dublin being the main port of departure.

A Coruña and Ferrol became the main starting points for pilgrims arriving from Northern Europe. Pilgrim hospitals along the route attest to their significance, records showing the deaths of pilgrims from England and elsewhere attest to their wide popularity during the medieval period. These port cities of Spain, being the closest to England, naturally drew pilgrims, people and produce going in the *opposite* direction. There is an interesting historical account of Prince Philip (later *King Felipe II)* journeying as a pilgrim to Santiago and continuing along the Camino Inglés on his way to A Coruña, where he set sail for England in July 1554 to marry Mary Tudor daughter of Henry VIII and Catherine of Aragon. The marriage lasted only 4 years, allowing him time to change his mind about the English and to instigate the Armada which set sail from A Coruña in 1588. We can see the houses where he stayed in A Calle (stage 5) & Sarandón (stage 6a).

The Protestant reformation in England caused a sudden and sharp decline in pilgrim numbers. While the challenge to Papal authority began in 1517 with Martin Luther it was in 1534 that Henry VIII declared he, not the Pope, was head of the Church of England. In the succeeding years Henry began to close down monasteries and outlawed pilgrimages, and the camino Inglés became moribund and all but forgotten until relatively recently.

Walking Today: The late 20th century has seen a revival of pilgrimage all across Spain including the Camino Inglés. In the year 2000 only 98 Pilgrims received a Compostela having walked the Camino Inglés but in 2023 this number increased to *24,093*! All were walkers as Inglés is less than the 200 km required for cyclists. Recent years have seen new private and municipal albergues opened and others refurbished. More cafés and shops are opening every year and the Xunta have invested significantly in waymarking, all of which has added to the accessibility of this route.

Of the two starting points the route from Ferrol (117.1 km from Santiago) sees the bulk of pilgrim traffic 96%. The 74.9 km journey from A Coruña, falling short of the distance required to apply for a compostela, was the recorded starting point for only 2.4% of pilgrims last year. However, recent agreement with the Pilgrim office in Santiago may well see a change in this trend. *Pilgrims walking from A Coruña can now apply for a Compostela if they can show evidence they have walked an additional 25+ km* before arriving. A letter from your local church or confraternity will suffice. If you are coming from the UK you can contact the Confraternity of St. James: *www.csj.org.uk* or the British Pilgrimage Trust: *www.britishpilgrimage.org* for details of available pilgrim routes. Pilgrims from Ireland can contact the Camino Society Ireland: *www.caminosociety.com* who issue a Celtic Compostela.

Given the historical links with Ireland it should, perhaps, come as no surprise that enthusiasm and support for this *Celtic Camino* is particularly strong within the Irish pilgrim community. The Camino Society Ireland have been issuing Celtic Compostelas for some time now but their work to support, encourage and make accessible caminos within Ireland is ever growing. In 2023 the Bray Camino was officially inaugurated, with a delegation from both Galicia and Ireland unveiling the first official *majones* on Irish soil (see photo). In a powerful and profound act of *meitheal* (the cooperation of neighbours) this camino includes both the Catholic and Protestant churches along its path. These churches welcome pilgrims of either faith or none, providing a warm welcome and stamps for those who call in. The route follows the coast from Bray to Dublin, finishing at St James Church, near St James Gate (the historic departure point for pilgrims travelling to Spain by sea). Details of this route and others are available on the Camino Society Ireland website and by visiting their information centre within St James Church.

While the route from Ferrol boasts beautiful stretches along the wide open *rías*, through green countryside and passing charming towns, the route from A Coruña has not only struggled to attract pilgrims due to being under 100 km. The long and at times arduous path through the cities suburbs has not been a huge draw to pilgrims. However, this guide includes a delightful green alternative route following the coast and river to Sigrás. This makes the route considerably more appealing and we hope will help to encourage pilgrims to explore all of the treasures and delights that the A Coruña road has to offer.

One of these is the chance to visit the only site along the many caminos with an alleged connection to the life of Jesus. On the recommended alternative route out of A Coruña is a short (20 minute) detour to Cambre that houses one of the legendary containers used in Christ's first miracle; the changing of water into wine at the wedding in Cana in Galilee (see stage 1a) allegedly bought back from the Holy Land by a Templar knight. Perhaps, in time, this itinerary will become the *Camino de Cristo*. It would be a fitting epithet for this modest detour through shaded woodland to the church of Santa Maria. *(The cathedral in Lugo also claims one of the containers).* There is also an opportunity to *include both routes as one camino*. If you start in Ferrol then, when arriving in Hospital de Bruma, take the regular bus direct to A Coruña and walk back to Bruma before continuing the journey to Santiago.

The *Camiño de San Andrés de Teixido:* Crossing the Camino Inglés at a number of points is the pilgrimage route of St Andrew *San Andrés* leading to his chapel in Teixido, a place not unlike Finisterre where Celtic mythology suggests that the veil between the worlds is thin and the doorway to the otherworld more open. Legend tells us that San Andrés was shipwrecked off the coast of Teixido. God helped him to escape with his life and in gratitude San Andrés built a chapel for both the living and the dead to visit. It was believed that those who did not visit the chapel in their present life would have to return and visit the chapel in a reptilian body! There are several starting points for this route which coincide with the Camino Inglés. The historic start point is the *Igrexa y Monasterio de San Martin de Xubia* in Narón (stage 1). Other routes cross at Miño and Betanzos where you may see the red fish – symbol for this route. More info at *www.caminoasanandres.com*

Galicia: Historical Snapshot, Brief Chronology and Mythology:

What follows is not a scholarly or historical treatise. It is included as a context in which to better understand the land we pass through and its people. It appears on a yellow panel so you can easily skip this section if you have read it in one of the other guidebooks or if it is of no interest. Here belief and legend should not be confused with the truth to which they point. We may miss the point entirely if we only take the literal view and try and drag the mystical into the factual.

• *Megalithic period c. 4000 B.C.*

We know little of the Neolithic peoples who inhabited the western fringes of Europe. However, evidence of their stonework can be found all over Galicia and goes back 6,000 years as seen in the petroglyphs and rock art of 4,000 B.C. and the dolmens *mamoas* of the same period. These mega-monuments are dotted all around Galicia. This megalithic culture was deeply religious in nature and left a powerful impact on the peoples who followed.

• *Early Celtic period c. 1000 B.C.*

Central European Celts travelled to and settled in western Spain, these Celti-Iberians were the forebears of the Celtic Nerios peoples who came to inhabit Galicia centuries before the Roman occupation. Remains of their Celtic villages *castros* can still be found, fortified villages built in a circular formation, usually occupied some elevated ground or hillock. We pass one of the largest **Eira dos Mouros** (see stage 4, p.55). Due to the extensive mineral deposits of Galicia Celtic bronze and gold artefacts from this area can still be seen in museums across Europe.

Galician Celts trace their mythic lineage to the king of Scythia in the Black sea area where the Druid Caichar had a vision in which he saw them travelling west to found Galicia and Ireland. The first Gaelic colony was established in Galicia under Brath and his son Breogán the latter becoming the legendary hero who founded Brigantium (present day A Coruña) entering folklore and the national anthem of Galicia in the process, *'Wake up from your dreams, home of Breogán.'* His grandson became King Milesius after whom the Celtic Milesians were named. It is generally accepted that the first Celts to settle in Ireland were Milesians from Galicia. Early Christian monks then extended the Celtic lineage 36 generations back to link it with the biblical Adam!

• *Early Christian Period c. 40 A.D*

While there may be no historical evidence to support the view that St. James preached in Galicia there are many anecdotal references to that effect. There are a depressing number of images of Santiago Matamoros (slayer of the Moors) along the Camino Inglés but the more benign **Santiago Peregrino**

is also found, (here> from the church of Santiago in Betanzos). It seems St. James sailed to Galicia to preach Christ's message, his body was then returned after his martyrdom in Jerusalem around 40 A.D. It is reasonable to assume that he would have sought to bring the Christian message to areas of spiritual significance and Finisterre was one of the most significant spiritual sites in the world at that time. It was also accessible, being directly on the sea route from Palestine.

• *Early Roman period 100 B.C.*

By the end of the 1st century the Romans controlled most of the southern Iberian peninsular naming the province *Hispania Ulterior* (including *Gallaecia*). In 61 BC Julius Caesar conducted naval expeditions along the coast, ultimately wrested control of the Atlantic seaboard from the Phoenicians. In 136 the proconsul Decimus Junius Brutus led his legions across the Lima and Minho rivers to enter Gallaecia for the first time. He met resistance from the fierce inhabitants but also from his own men wary of crossing the river *Lima* thought to represent one of the rivers of Hades – the river of forgetfulness *Lethe*. Brutus was the first Roman general to make it to Finisterre 'by road'. He was reputedly mesmerised at the way the sea 'drank up' the sun and was predisposed to the pagan worship centred on the Phoenician Altar to the Sun *Ara Solis* (facing west to the 'Land of Eternal Youth' *Tir-na-Nóg*). Roman perseverance in conquering this corner of Hispania was, however, primarily due to its rich mining potential. Gold was found in small quantities in Galicia long before the Romans turned production along the Sil valley (on the ***Camino Invierno*** *)* into the largest goldmines in the Empire.

• *The Middle Ages 476 – 1453*

After the fall of the Roman Empire in 476 CE the north-western province (now Galicia) was ruled by the Vandals, Suevi and Visigoths, descendants of the Germanic tribes that had overrun Roman Hispania forcing its collapse. It is hard to believe (and much misunderstood) but the Moorish 'invasion' of the Iberian peninsula in 711 was actually by invitation from the

squabbling Visigothic nobles to help in their domestic feuds. The Umayyad Muslims obliged and so the invasion by invitation began. *(photo> the Mihrab & Qibla facing Mecca in the mosque (now cathedral) at Córdoba built by Abd al-Rahmanm I with its iconic Mozarabic arch).* Muslim forces quickly moved north to conquer the whole peninsular, capturing the bells of Santiago cathedral along the way and taking them to Granada. But Galicia proved impossible to control and Islamic rule here lasted only a few decades. It was to take another 700 years before the re-conquest was complete in the south – and the bells returned to Santiago.

No sketch of Spanish history would be complete without looking at the contribution of the Templar knights, both to the reconquest *reconquista* of the Iberian peninsular but also its subsequent support of the pilgrimage routes to Santiago. These warrior monks originated in Jerusalem in 1118 A.D with a vow to 'protect pilgrims on  the roads leading to Jerusalem' from their headquarters in part of the original Solomon's Temple. After the Holy Land was 'lost' to Islam their focus turned to the reconquest of Spain. This is when the powerful and terrifying image of St. James the Moorslayer *Santiago Matamoros* first appeared (see photo above). Alongside images of the Knights Templar, mounted on their own chargers, dressed in white tunics emblazoned with the Templar Cross. Once the reconquest was complete the Knights switched their role to protecting pilgrims, including those on the camino Inglés. A major presence was around O Burgo on the route from A Coruña (see stage 1a / Cambre page 68). In 1307 the French monarch Philippe IV moved against the Knights in an attempt to purloin their considerable fortunes to alleviate his own financial problems. The Order 'blended' into the Hospitallers.

• The Catholic Monarchs 1469 – 1516

The marriage in 1469 of Isabella I of Castille and Fernando II of Aragón saw the merging of two of the most powerful kingdoms in Spain. The title Catholic Monarchs *los Reyes Católicos* was bestowed by Pope Alexander VI with an eye to unifying Spain under Roman Catholicism. This was finally achieved after the conquest of Granada in 1492, the same year Columbus 'discovered' the Americas. This period saw the expulsion or massacre of non-Catholics under the horrifying Spanish Inquisition. Isabella is also remembered for her more beneficent activities such as the building of the pilgrim hospital in Santiago, now the *parador Hostal Dos Reis Católicos* – reputedly the oldest hotel in the world in continuous occupation for that purpose.

• The War(s) of Independence 1807 – 1814

Despite its remote location, Galicia was not spared the effects of the War of Independence 'Peninsular War' (1807–1814) when forces of Napoleon clashed with Bourbon Spain for control of the Iberian Peninsula, ransacking many of the villages we pass through. It began when the French and Spanish invaded Portugal in 1807 and escalated the following year when France turned on its former ally Spain and lasted until Napoleon was defeated in 1814. The Peninsular War overlaps with the Spanish War of Independence *Guerra de la Independencia Española* which began with the uprising on 2 May 1808 *Dos de Mayo*. (See p.59 for details of the death of Sir John Moor who died defending A Coruña against the French in 1809).

• *The Carlist Wars & First Spanish Republic 1833 – 1876*

Next came the Carlist Wars between Carlos V and his followers fighting for absolutist Monarchy and Catholicism against the forces of liberalism and republicanism. Towards the end of the 3rd Carlist war the first Spanish Republic was proclaimed in 1873. Again the remoteness of Galicia was no bar to its involvement in anti-monarchist activities. Indeed its resistance to any outside interference continues to this day.

No introduction to Galicia would be complete without mention of Castelao who was born in Rianxo (20 km west of Padrón) in 1886 and who died in Buenos Aires in 1950. Identified as a founding father of Galician nationalism he was, nevertheless, decidedly pro-European writing in *Sempre en Galiza* that one of his dreams was to, 'see the emergence of a United States of Europe'. He presented the idea of an independent Galician State *Estatuto de Galicia* to the Spanish Parliament in the same year that General Franco appeared on the political scene. Despite various initiatives to earn independence for Galicia it was not until 1981 that it achieved a measure of autonomy, being recognised as a separate autonomous region in that year.

• *The Spanish Civil War 1936 –1939 & Franco Period.*

General Franco was born in Ferrol in 1892 and in 1936 he seized power leading to one of the bloodiest civil wars in history, the effects of which can still be felt today despite the 'Pact of Forgetting' *Pacto del Olvido*. This was a decision by all parties to the conflict to avoid having to deal with the horrifying legacy of Fascism under Franco after his death in 1975. The Pact attempted to transition from an autocratic to democratic rule of law without recriminations for the countless thousands killed summarily and buried in unmarked graves throughout Spain. While suppression of painful memories helped in national reconciliation at that time – these memories remain close to the surface and there is a growing sense within Spain today that it should now take a more honest and open look at the injustices of that period.

The Spanish Civil War *Guerra Civil Española* pitted Republicans (with Communist and Socialist sympathies), against the Nationalists a predominantly conservative Catholic and Fascist grouping led by General Francisco Franco. Fascism prevailed not least owing to the intervention of Nazi Germany and Fascist Italy who provided weapons, soldiers and air bombardment (Guernica). This struggle between democracy and fascism for the soul of Spain was to last until Franco's death in 1975.

• *Galicia Today 1975 – 2020*

After Franco's death King Carlos nominally succeeded and appointed political reformist Adolfo Suárez to form a government. In 1982 the Spanish Socialist Workers' Party *Partido Socialista Obrero Español* **PSOE** won a sweeping victory under Felipe González who successfully steered Spain into full membership of the EEC in 1986. In 1996 José María Aznar, leader of the centre-right People's Party *Partido Popular* **PP** won a narrow mandate but in 2002 the oil tanker Prestige ran into a storm off Finisterre and the ensuing ecological catastrophe sank not only the livelihood of scores of Galician fisherman but, in due time, the right wing government as well resulting in a popular cry up and down the country of 'never again' *nunca maís*. With the socialist's back in power under José Luis Rodríguez Zapatero the government set in motion an immediate change in foreign policy and, more controversially, a sudden but decisive shift from a conservative Catholic to a liberal secular society that led to one newspaper headline, *'Church and State square up in struggle for the spirit of Spain.'* ... The fine balance between secular and religious Spain and the ever changing alliances and coalitions between the socialist and conservative parties in government continue on, and yet, seemingly immune to all these social and political upheavals, the *Caminos* go quietly about their gentle spirit of transformation.

Galician Culture: The flowering of Galician art that took place under Alfonso VII and Ferdinand II (kings of Galicia until it was absorbed into León and Castille under Ferdinand III) saw the completion of the great cathedrals of Ourense, Lugo and Tui, as well as Santiago. However, between the three great powers comprising the Catholic monarchy, the Aristocracy and Castille; Galician art, culture and language were greatly diluted. Indeed while the French Way *Camino Francés* introduced wonderfully inspiring European art and artisans to towns all along the route to Santiago, it had the effect of diminishing the Celtic influences within Galicia.

Galician Language: The distinctive language of Galicia *Gallego* is still widely used today. The language institute estimates that 94% of the population understand it, while 88% can speak it. Gallego belongs to the Iberian Romance group of languages with some common aspects with Portuguese. Phrase books between Spanish *Castellano* Galician *Gallego* and English are difficult to find but one of the more obvious differences is the substitution of the Spanish J – hard as in Junta (pron: **kh**unta) as opposed to the softer Galego Xunta (pron: **sh**unta). Here are a few common phrases to help distinguish one from the other:

The Jacobean Way	Del Camino Jacobeo	Do Camiño Xacobeo
Fountains of Galicia	Las Fuentes de Galicia	Das Fontes de Galiza
The Botanical garden	El Jardin Botanico	O Xardín Botánico
Collegiate church	Colegiata Iglesia	Colexiata Igrexa
Below the main Square	Bajo el plaza mayor	Debaixo do praza maior

The Revival *Rexurdimento* of Galician language and literature in the 19th century was spearheaded with the publication in 1863 of *Cantares Gallegos* by the incomparable Galician poetess, Rosalía Castro. The Revival reached its zenith in the 1880's with the publication of many illuminating Galician texts such as *Follas Novas* also by Rosalía Castro, *Saudades Galegas* by Lamas de Carvajal and *Queixumes dos Pinos* by Eduardo Pondal. Galicia's culture has been kept alive as much by its exiles, political and economic, as by those that remained behind. The unofficial anthem of Galicia, The Pines *Os Pinos* was written and first sung in South America where it urged the Galician people to awaken from the yoke of servitude into freedom: *'Listen to the voices of the murmuring pines which is none other than the voices of the Galician people.'* However, even the pine trees seem under threat from the imported eucalyptus that has taken over large swathes of the countryside.

The fruits of this revival can be tasted, nonetheless, throughout Galicia today. You may well hear the swirl of the traditional Galician bagpipes *Gaita* in the bars of Santiago or Ferrol or at one of its many festivals and fairs that take place throughout the year. Many of these are based on the ancient Celtic celebration of the seasons particularly at the equinoxes and the summer and winter solstices. The short pilgrimages to local shrines *romerías* endorse the deeply held religious values of the people of Galicia but drawing ever larger crowds are the secular festivals such as the Night of the Templars *Noche Templaria* which is, in fact, a 5 day celebration of tradtional markets, parades, music events and firework shows.

Galician Nationalism appears to be born more out of a deep pride in its traditions, rather than a need to overthrow a culture that has been imposed from outside. This is not unlike other Celtic cultures that have found themselves marginalised on the Western fringes of Europe. We demean Galicia and ourselves by stereotyping popular Spanish culture onto her. This is not the Spain of castanets, paella and Rioja wines. Her identity is clearly Celtic with *gaitas, mariscos* and *Albariño* wines predominating – all of which are a cause of justified pride.

This guidebook provides you with essential information in a concise format. The maps have been designed so you can instantly see how far it is to the next place of interest. Distances on the maps correspond to those in the text and are generally spaced at around 3 km intervals (approximately 1 hour of walking at an average pace). For clarity and accuracy each stage begins and ends at the front door of a specified pilgrim hostel or other defined 'end point'. Maps are one directional *to* Santiago; if you intend to walk the route 'in reverse' source conventional maps. The camino path is shown as follows:

❶ ●●●● **Main Route** (carrying around 80% of pilgrims) generally follows the most direct path and is indicated by a line of yellow dots symbolic of the yellow arrows / shells that will be your guide throughout the journey. Distances along this route are shown in **blue.**

❷ ●●●● **Scenic Routes** are generally not waymarked on the ground but provide a "greener" alternative to the main route. These quieter paths are shown with **green** dots indicating the natural landscape they travel through. Any text appears on a green panel.

❸ ●●●● **Detours** to places of special interest are shown with **turquoise** dots and the text appears on a turquoise panel.

❹ ●●●● **Road Routes** follow on or close to asphalt roads and are marked with **grey** dots symbolising asphalt.

Waymarks along the Camino Inglés are now extensive. These signs pointing our way come in a variety of forms, including the famous yellow arrows *flechas amrillas* and scallop shells in various designs. Spotting them will become second nature but stay present and focused especially at points shown with a [!]. If you find yourself temporarily off-course be careful when asking directions as locals are not always familiar with the waymarked paths and may direct you along public roads – it is often best to re-trace your steps until you pick up the waymarks again.

A **Sun-Compass** has been provided on each map as an aid to orientation. Should you become 'lost' this will help you to re-orientate. Even in poor weather we can generally tell the direction of the sun so, for example, if you are walking from Bruma to Sigüeiro you are heading South and the morning sun will be on your left (east). At midday you will be walking towards the sun (south) and by late afternoon the sun will be on your right (west). If, for example, you find yourself in the afternoon with the sun consistently on your left – stop and re-assess.

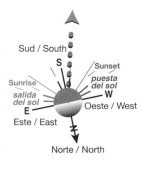

Distances: The maps have been designed to show relevant information only and are therefore not strictly to scale – instead accurate distances are given between each point marked on the map and this corresponds to the text for ease of reference. Distances in between these points are shown bracketed in the text as follows: [**1.0** km] + [**0.2** km] add up to the boxed figure in blue `1.2 km` Villages in Spain, particularly Galicia, can tend to straggle without a defined centre and even the local church is frequently located outside the actual town so distances are measured to an albergue or other clearly defined feature.

Distance and Pace: The following chart may help establish the distance you can accomplish each day. Time must also be adjusted depending on the ***cumulative*** **ascent** of that stage. This 'additional' time is given for each stage (± *1 ¼ hr*) and based loosely on the Naismith rule of 10 minutes for every 100 metres climbed.

Fitness Level	Speed	Time	*20km*	*25km*	*30km*	*35km*
			The distances (above) in kilometres			
			will take the time (below) in hours			
Fast walker	5 kph	12 min /km	**4.0***hr*	**5.0***hr*	**6.0***hr*	**7.0***hr*
Average pace	4 kph	15 min /km	**5.0***hr*	**6.3***hr*	**7.5**hr	**8.6***hr*
Leisurely pace	3 kph	20 min /km	**6.6***hr*	**8.3***hr*	—	—

Note that pace will *decrease,* often substantially, towards the end of a day. That is why pilgrims sometimes question the measurements given for the *last* section suggesting it was *double* the distance indicated (it took twice as long as expected). They were right about the time but not the distance!

Language: Text and place names are provided in *Galego* unless they appear 'on the ground' in Spanish. The Church of St. John may, therefore, appear as *Iglesia San Juan* or *Igrexa San Xoán.*

Contour Guides are shown for each day. This will give you a thumbnail sketch of the day's terrain and help you prepare for the uphill stretches and anticipate the downhill ones. They are drawn to an exaggerated scale to emphasise steep inclines.

Abbreviations: The following abbreviations are used throughout the text:
<left means *turn* left – (left) means *on* your left. right> *turn* right etc.

s/o = continue straight on	adj. = adjoing / adjacent
c. = circa (about)	incl. = including
c/ = Calle	r/ = Rua
¶ = Restaurant	*V.* = Vegetarian
XII^th^c / 12th century.	[m] mobile phone number
[?] indicates an option.	[⌂] *fuente* drinking font.

[!] = Attention! Indicates dangerous road / steep descents / poor waymarking.

Accommodation pricing: €pp = per person / incl. = including breakfast)
€25 – 40 = price for single room – price for double room.

Pilgrim Passport *Credencial***:** Official pilgrim hostels are reserved exclusively for pilgrims on the camino who must have a pilgrim passport *credencial* that has been stamped along the way. These passports are available from your local confraternity

(see list of addresses at the back - consider joining and supporting these organisations that do so much for the camino). If you have been unable to acquire a credencial before travelling – don't worry as they are available in Ferrol or A Coruña. To apply for a *Compostela* you need to have your credencial stamped twice daily and walk at least100km (for details of how to qualify for a Compostela when walking from A Coruña see p.8). Stamps *sellos* are readily available from churches, hostels, hotels, even bars.

Pilgrim hostels *albergues de peregrinos* vary in what they provide but lodging is usually in bunk beds with additional overflow space on mattresses *colchonetas*. Number of beds and number of dormitories is shown in brackets *[8÷2] / [40÷1]* (simple division will provide an idea of density!) Xunta / municipal hostels provide a kitchen with basic cooking equipment and a dining / sitting area. Opening times vary depending on the time of year but most are generally cleaned and open again from early afternoon (14:00) to welcome pilgrims. You cannot reserve a bed in a Xunta albergue in advance and phone numbers are provided for emergency calls or to check availability outside the normal seasons (most are open all year but can close for holidays or maintenance purposes). Private albergues are also increasing available, while bunk beds are still the norm these private hostels often have additional private rooms shown as follows (*+4* €35) and it is generally possible to reserve your bed in a private hostel in advance.

Costs: Xunta *Xun.* albergues cost €10 per night with private albergues *Priv.* ranging from €12- €20. This provides us with a bunk bed and use of a hot shower. Many offer additional facilities such as use of washing and drying machines for a small charge and many private hostals also provide individual rooms from €30+. Hotels •*H*, hostales •*Hs*, pensiónes •*P* or casa rurales •*CR* literally 'rural house' (a type of up-market B&B) vary widely from €25 - €100+ depending on facilities and season. Number of rooms (*x2* versus *x102*) indicates type and likely facilities on offer. Allow for a basic minimum €30 a day to include overnight stay at a Xunta hostel and remainder for food and drink. Some hostels provide a communal dinner and most have a basic kitchen *cocina* where a meal can be prepared. Alternatively most locations have one or more restaurants to choose from. Pilgrim menus *menú peregrino* may be available for around €10 incl. wine. If you want to indulge in the wonderful seafood *mariscos* available in Galicia and accompany this with the delightful local *Albariño* wines expect to double or treble the basic cost! *Note: not all businesses accept card payments so it is advisable to carry some cash.*

Safety: The camino offers a remarkably safe environment in an inherently unsafe world. When viewed in this context few cases of crime or harassment are reported but they have been known to occur. If you are a solo pilgrim and feel unsafe, keep other pilgrims in sight or ask to walk with someone until you feel comfortable again. In the event of an emergency or to report an incident the EU wide emergency number is **112**. Road traffic is the major safety concern and extra vigilance is needed while on or crossing roadways.

Mobile Phones: Recent years have seen an exponential rise in mobile phone use, impacting our individual and collective experience. The constant connectivity with our familiar *outer* world can keep us disconnected from the expansiveness of our *inner* world and the camaraderie of our 'camino family'. While most of us will carry a mobile phone for safety and practicality perhaps we can, collectively, be more conscious about how and when we use them. For those wishing to consider this further see: *www.walkingtopresence.com*

Some Statistics: While we can never know the actual number of pilgrims who arrive into Santiago each year we do know from records kept at the Pilgrim Office *www.oficinadelperegrino.com* that a total 446,046 pilgrims collected a Compostela in 2023. Of these *24,093* walked the Camino Inglés, with *22,953 starting in Ferrol (96%) 577 in A Coruña (2.4%) and 70 in Ireland.*

Of all recorded pilgrims on the caminos 40% gave a religious reason for their journey and 60% "religious or other". The majority (79%) were between the ages of 18 and 65. Women outnumbered men (53%). 93% arrived on foot, 5% by bicycle, 606 on horseback, 276 by boat and 198 by wheelchair.

When to go: Spring can be wet and windy but the route is relatively quiet with early flowers appearing. Summer is often busier and can be very hot, with tourists creating a lively atmosphere but also adding pressure to services and accommodation. Autumn usually provides the most stable weather with harvesting adding to the colour and celebrations of the countryside. Winter is solitary and cold with reduced daylight hours for walking and some hostels will be closed. Pilgrims are found on the route throughout the year, the best time for *you* to go will be a matter of personal preference.

Pilgrims per month per camino

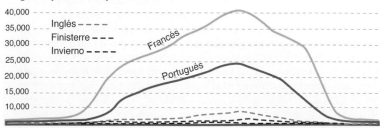

Preparation – A Quick Guide:

❶ **Practical Considerations:**

• **When?** Spring is often wet and windy but the route is relatively quiet with early flowers appearing. Summer is busy and hot and hostels are often full. Autumn usually provides the most stable weather with harvesting adding to the colour and celebrations of the countryside. Winter is solitary and cold with reduced daylight hours for walking and some hostels will be closed.

• **How long?** El Ferrol to Santiago is 117.1 km can be walked easily in 6 days (av. 19.5 km per day) or 5 days (av. 23.4 km per day). Add 2 extra days to include A Coruña. Allow 4 days to walk straight from A Coruña to Santiago. Interim lodging allows each stage to be varied according to differing abilities, pace, preferences and needs. (See p.17).

❷ **Preparation – Outer: what do I need to take...**
• Buy your boots in time to walk them in before you go.
• Pack a Poncho – Galicia is notorious for its downpours.
• Bring a hat – sunstroke is painful and can be dangerous.
• Look again if your backpack weighs more than 10 kilos.

If this is your first pilgrimage more comprehensive notes on preparation and packing are available at _www.caminoguides.com_

... _and_ **consider leaving behind.**

• Books, except this one – all the maps and promptings you need are included.
• Extras, Galicia has shops if you need to replace something.
• Everything that is superfluous for pilgrimage. Take time to reflect carefully on this point as it can form the basis of our questioning of what is really important in our life and spiritual awakening. We have become reliant, even addicted, to so many extraneous 'things'. We need to de-clutter if we are to clear space for what truly matters in our lives.

❸ **Language:** learn at least some basic phrases now, _before_ you go.

❹ **Pilgrim Passport:** Get a _credencial_ from your local confraternity (see p.18 for details and p.90 for list of local confraternities).

❺ **Protocol:** Have consideration for the needs of your fellow pilgrims, gratitude for your hosts and take care of nature and the Landscape Temple.

❻ **Prayer:** May my every step be a prayer for peace and loving kindness.

❼ **Preparation** _Inner_**:** Why is my purpose for walking the camino? (p.22)

Total km   Total distance for stage
equiv.   Adjusted for cumulative climb (each 100m vertical +10 mins)

(850m) **Alto** ▲   Contours / High point of each stage

< Ⓐ Ⓗ >   Intermediate accommodation ❷ (*often less busy / quieter*)

3.5 ▶   Precise distance between points (3.5 km = ± 1 hour)

━● 50m > / ^ / <   Interim distances 50m right> / s/o=straight on^ / <left

....   Natural path / forest track / gravel *senda*

━━━━━━━   Quiet country lane (asphalt)

━━━○━━━   Secondary road (*grey*: asphalt) / Roundabout *rotonda*

━━N-11━━   Main road [N-] *Nacional* (*red*: additional traffic and hazard)

━━A-1━━   Motorway *autopista* (*blue*: conventional motorway colour)

++++++++●   Railway *ferrocarril* / Station *estación*

● ● ● ● ● ●   Main Waymarked route (*yellow*: ± 80% of pilgrims)

● ● ● ● ● ●   Alternative Scenic route (*green*: more remote / less pilgrims)

● ● ● ● ● ●   Alternative road route (*grey*: more asphalt & traffic)

● ● ● ● ● ●   Optional detour *desvío* (*turquoise:* to point of interest)

▬▬▬▬▬   Primary Path of pilgrimage (***purple***: inner path of Soul)

🅧 ❓ ❶   Crossing *cruce* / Option *opción* / Extra care *¡cuidado!*

🌾 ☀ 🗼   Windmill *molino* / Viewpoint *punto de vista* / Radio mast

▪━▪/▪   National boundary / Provincial boundary *límite provincial*

∼/∼   River *río* / Riverlet Stream *arroyo / rego*

⬭/⬭   Sea or lake *Mar o lago* / Woodland *bosques*

♱ ♱ ✝   Church *iglesia* / Chapel *capilla* / Wayside cross *cruceiro*

🄵 ☕ 🅼   Drinking font *fuente* [🚰] / Café-Bar 🍴 / Shop (*mini*)*mercado* 🛒

🍴 *menú V.*   Restaurant / *menú peregrino* / *V. Vegetariano(a)*

🄸 🏛 ✕   Tourist office ❶ *turismo* / Manor house *pazo* / Rest area *picnic*

➕ ⊕ ✉   Pharmacy *farmacia* / Hospital / Post office *correos*

⊕ 🚌 ⛽   Airport / Bus station *estación de autobús / gasolinera*

⁙ *XIIc.*   Ancient monument / 12th century

🄷 🄿 🄲   Hotels •*H-H*˙€30-90 / Pension •*P*˙€20-35 / •*CR (B&B)* €35-75

x12 €35-45   Number of private rooms *x12* €40(single)-50 (double) *approx*

🄷 🄰 🄰   *Off* route lodging / 🄰 Reported closed - check for updates

🄰❶❷ 🄹   Pilgrim hostel(s) *Albergue* ●*Alb.* + Youth hostel ●*Juventude*

[32]   Number of bed spaces (usually bunk beds *literas*) €10-€18

[÷4] +12   ÷ number of dormitories / *+12* number of private rooms €30+

Par.   Parish hostel *Parroquial* donation *donativo* / €5

Conv.   Convent or monastery hostel *donativo* / €5

Mun/ Xunta   Municipal hostel €8+ / Galician government *Xunta* €10

Asoc.   Association hostel €10+

Priv. (*)   Private hostel (network*) €10-18+
   [all prices average (low season) for comparison purposes only]

p.55   Town plan *plan de la ciudad* with page number

(Pop.– Alt. m)   Town population – altitude in metres

▭   City suburbs / outskirts *afueras* (*grey*)
   Historical centre *centro histórico / barrio antiguo* (*brown*)

SELF-ASSESSMENT *INNER WAYMARKS These notes appear on a purple panel so you can easily skip over if they are of no interest or benefit to you.*

This self-assessment questionnaire is designed to encourage us to reflect on our life purpose and direction. We can view it as a snapshot of this moment in our evolving life-story. In the busyness that surrounds us we often fail to take stock of where we are headed. Authors of our unfolding drama and we can rewrite the script anytime we choose. Our next steps are up to us...

You might find it useful to initially answer these questions in quick succession as this may allow a more intuitive response. Afterwards, you can reflect more deeply and check if your intellectual answers confirm these, change them or bring in other insights. Download copies of the questionnaire from the *Camino Guides* website and repeat the exercise on your return and again in (say) 6 months time. This way we can compare results and ensure we follow through on any insights and commitments that come to us while walking the camino.

☐ How do I differentiate pilgrimage from a long distance walk?
☐ How do I define spirituality – what does it mean to me?
☐ How is my spirituality expressed at home and at work?

☐ What do I see as the primary purpose of my life?
☐ Am I working consciously towards fulfilling that purpose?
☐ How clear am I on my goal and the right direction for me at this time?
☐ How will I recognise my resistance to any changes in my life that may be required in order to reach my goal?

☐ When did I first become aware of a desire to take time-out?
☐ What prompted me originally to go on the camino de Santiago?
☐ Did the prompt come from something that I felt needed changing?
☐ Make a list of what appears to be blocking any change from happening.

☐ What help might I need on a practical, emotional and spiritual level?
☐ How will I recognise the right help or correct answer?
☐ What are the likely challenges in working towards my unique potential?
☐ What are my next steps towards fulfilling that potential?

How aware are you of the following? Score yourself on a level of 1 – 10 and compare these scores again on your return from the camino.

☐ Awareness of my inner spiritual world and its reality.
☐ Clarity on what inspires me and the capacity to live my passion.
☐ Confidence to follow my intuitive sense of the 'right' direction.
☐ Ability to recognise my resistance and patterns of defence.
☐ Ease with asking for and receiving support from others.

Take time to prepare a purpose for this pilgrimage and complete the self-assessment questionnaire. We would benefit by starting from the basis that we are essentially spiritual beings on a human journey. We came to learn some lesson and this pilgrimage affords an opportunity to find out what that is. Ask for help and expect it – it's there, now, waiting for us.

REFLECTIONS:

"I am doing the camino once again, looking for something I left behind or perhaps never found. It's like coming home." Notes from a pilgrim from New Mexico recorded in the Pilgrims book on the first stage of the journey. What are your reflections for this day?

_____
_____
_____
_____
_____
_____
_____
_____
_____
_____
_____
_____
_____
_____
_____
_____
_____
_____
_____
_____
_____
_____
_____
_____
_____
_____
_____
_____
_____
_____

Marina De Ferrol *Puerto Deportivo*
Camino Inglés start point

TRAVEL to/from **Santiago:**

AIR: *Direct flights to Santiago:* •*Easyjet* from London Gatwick, Geneva & Basle. •*Ryanair* from London Stansted, Frankfurt & Milan. •*Vueling* from London, Paris, Brussels, Amsterdam & Zurich. •*Aer Lingus* from Dublin (summer schedule). •*BA / Iberia* and other major airlines offer regular services throughout the year via various connecting airports in Spain, mainly Madrid. *Vueling* also fly direct from London to *A Coruña* and *Asturias*. Check other possibilities from / to nearby airports at A Coruña, Vigo, Porto – all of which have regular rail and bus connections to/from Santiago.

BUS: book online (paypal only) with **ALSA** _alsa.com_ direct services to Santiago from Madrid airport and other major cities within Spain.

RAIL: book online through Spanish rail network **RENFE** _renfe.com_ or **Rail Europe** _raileurope.co.uk_ direct services to Santiago from Madrid *Chamartin* and other major cities within Spain.

*Check public transport options for bus and rail with _www.rome2rio.com_*

FERRY: Travelling by sea provides a chance to acclimatise slowly and reduce our carbon footprint. Check Brittany Ferries: Portsmouth & Plymouth to Santander _brittany-ferries.co.uk_ with onward travel to Santiago by bus or rail.

TRAVEL *to/from* **FERROL:** Monbus run a regular (hourly) service from Santiago to Ferrol from the main bus station. Tickets cost around €10 with journey time of approx 1¼ hours. *[**Note:** some buses go via A Coruña with a journey time of 2¼ hours – check schedules].* Tickets can be bought from the bus station in Santiago or online at _www.monbus.com_ © +34 982 292 900. Train services run daily with tickets from €20 and a journey time of approx 2 hours. Tickets can be purchased from the train station or via _www.renfe.com_ *[For travel to/from A Coruña see p. 59].*

Travel Notes:

_____
_____
_____
_____
_____
_____
_____
_____
_____
_____
_____

CAMINO INGLÉS: FERROL TO SANTIAGO – 117.1 km (*72.7 ml*). The considerable increase in pilgrim numbers along this route has lead to significant investment in facilities and waymarking along it. Large sections of the route were re-directed and re-waymarked in 2017. Though the new waymarking is clear remnants of the old signage remains and so these old routes have been left in this guide to avoid possible confusion (in case you stray onto them by accident) and as alternative options. These original waymarkings will fade, however, and so these alternative routes are only recommended for those confident in navigation. Another source of potential confusion are the distances displayed on waymarks on the ground. It is impossible for these signs to comprehensively convey the multiple route choices and changes which account for the slight variations in reported distance. So please do not be perturbed if a sign on the ground indicates a distance that does not correspond exactly to that listed in this guide.

This guide is divided into 6 daily stages. However, some choose to join the first two relatively short stages together, walking directly from Ferrol to Pontedeume. Others choose to add an extra day (or two) to shorten the distance walked each day. We encourage you not to feel tied to the 6 stages we present if this does not serve you, and to use the interim accommodation available to create an itinerary that works for you.

While the overall distance of this route is not the longest of the many caminos, the Camino Inglés is by no means an easy option. The beautiful coastal landscape is far from flat and the undulating terrain continues as we head inland. But each arduous uphill climb is rewarded by its views and the charming towns and villages we pass through offer us many warm welcomes. The ubiquitous *eucalyptus,* that makes up the majority of the woodland we pass through, may not be native to the region but does provide shade from the sun and shelter from the wind and rain (which we may encounter at any time of year). So there is much to enjoy and be grateful for on this road to Santiago. Onwards and upwards *ultreia y suseia!*

FERROL, with its population of 70,000, is home to one of the largest Naval bases in Spain. It has been a centre for shipbuilding through the ages (see the award winning maritime museum of boat building *Exponav*) or apprciate the view of the navel harbour from the *Jardines de Herrera* (see photo>).

The city was the birthplace of Pablo Igrexas Posse founder of the Spanish Workers Party (PSOE) in 1879. The party was later outlawed by General Franco who, coincidently, was also born in Ferrol in 1892. Today Ferrol is a lively city, with many businesses lining its militarily straight streets.

Information: The new pilgrim & tourist office **❶** *Via Compostellam* ℭ 981 944 252 Paseo da Mariña (see photo>) adjoins the first waymark Km Zero and is open daily: Summer 08:30–14:00 & 17:00–19:00. / Winter 09:00–12:00 & 16:00–18:00.

❶ *Turismo Praza de España* (near the train and rail stations) ℭ 981 944 251 Summer 09:00–14:00 & 16:30–18:30. / Winter (variable) 09:30–12:30 & 16:00–18:00. The Spanish post office *Correos* also offer a range of services to pilgrims incl. luggage transfer and storage *www.elcaminoconcorreos.com/en*

● *Monumentos Históricos* *include:*

❶ *Monolito O Camiño do Inglés* starting point (*Km'0'*) (photo>) Paseo da Mariña, Porto de Curuxeiras adj. *Tourist office* and *Via Compostellam*

❷ *Baluarte San Juan XVIII* remains of original defensive wall with views over the harbour (see photo below).

❸ *Igrexa de San Francisco neoclásica XVIII*

❹ *Palacio Xeral e Xardíns de Herrera (adj. the Parador and with views over the naval base see photo oppposite.)*

❺ *Fuente de San Roque c.XVIII* with first familiar waymark *mojón*

❻ *Concatedral de San Julián (St. Xiao) c.XVIII* (see photo>). They provide a pilgrim passport *credencial* & stamp *sello*. Mass *misas* daily 11:00 & 19:30. Sun 11:00, 13:00 & 19:30.

Marina from *Baluarte San Juan XVIII*

❼ *Museo Naval* museum in former prison with models of iconic ships, nautical instruments & artillery. Rua Irmandiños ℂ 981 338 907 Open daily 09:30–13:30 adj. 09:30–13:30

❽ *Exponav Museo de Construcción Naval* Maritime museum at the Ferrol naval base with shipbuilding exhibits ℂ 981 359 682 Open daily (expt. Mon) 10:00–20:00.

Ferrol is a lively town with a variety of shops and a wide selection of bars, cafés and restaurants. Including ⅋ *O Camino do Inglés* ⅋ *Frank* ⅋ *Bodegón Bacoriñ* ⅋ *Pizzaria El Cantegril* ⅋ *O' Xantar* and 🍴 *Bla Bla* to name a few.

The increasing popularity of the Camino Inglés inspired the opening of the first Xunta albergue in town in 2023 ●*Alb.* **Ferrol** *Xunta.[60÷3]* €10 r/ Estrada Alta, 25. Impressive modern building near the harbour and route starting point, equipped with all necessary facilities.

Hoteles Centro: •*H*··· **El Suizo** *x34* €32-39 ℂ 981 300 400 *www. hotelsuizo.es* c/Dolores, 67 (rear facade Rua Real) popular with pilgrims (photo right). •*H* **Real Ferrol** *x45* €35-40 ℂ 981 351 586 *www.hotelrealferrol.com* c/Dolores 11. •*P* **La Parra** *x20* €13-22 ℂ 606 599 333 c/Carmen 19. •*H*· **Almendra** *x40* €25-40 ℂ 981 358 190 r/Almendra, 4. •*Hs* **Zahara** *x20* €25-40 ℂ 981 351 231 *www.hostalzahara.com* c/Pardo Bajo, 28. •*Hs*·· **La Frontera** *x19* €18-28 ℂ 881 953 036 r/ San Andrés 4. •*P*· **O'Choyo II** *x8* €18-35 ℂ 981 948 908 c/Carlos III, 67. •*H*··· **Parador de Ferrol** *x36* €75+(15% pilgrim discount) ℂ 981 356 720 Plaza C.Azarola Gresillón. •*H*···· **Almirante** *x98* €65-90 ℂ 981 333 073 c/ María, 2.

Other Lodging (Further out): •*H*···· **Gran de Ferrol** *x95* €49-55 ℂ 981 330 226 ctra/Castilla 75. •*H* **América** *x20é* €35-40 ℂ 981 370 208 76 c/Sánchez Calviño 70. •*H* **Silva** *x31* €28-€40 c/Rio Castro 42. •*Hs* **Ferrol** €20-34 c/ Sánchez Calviño 48. •*Hs* **Magallanes** *x14* €24-36 ctra/Castilla 401.

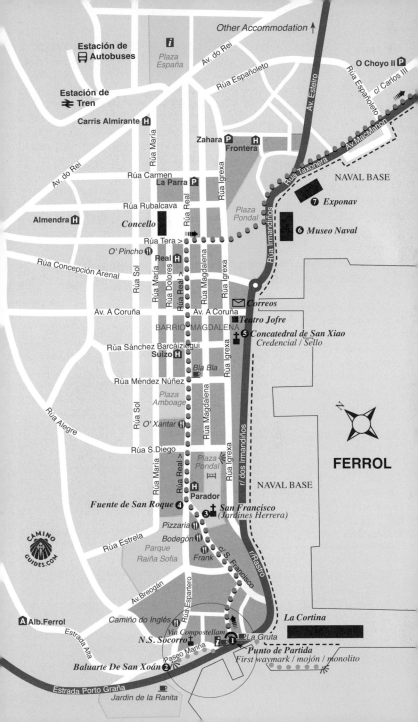

Other Accommodation ↑

Estación de 🚌 **Autobuses**

Plaza España

i

Av. do Rei

Rúa Españoleto

O Choyo II Ⓟ

Rúa Españoleto

c/ Carlos III

Estación de 🚊 **Tren**

Av. Esteiro

Carris Almirante Ⓗ

Rúa Maria

Av. MacMahon

Av. do Rei

Zahara Ⓟ
Ⓗ **Frontera**

NAVAL BASE

Rúa Taxonera

Rúa Carmen

La Parra Ⓟ

Rúa Igrexa

Rúa Rubalcava

Plaza Pondal

Ⓐ **Almendra** Ⓗ

Concello

Rúa Real

❼ *Exponav*

Rúa Irmandinos

Rúa Tera >

❻ *Museo Naval*

Rúa Concepción Arenal

O' Pincho Ⓗ

Real Ⓗ

Rúa Magdalena

Rúa Igrexa

Rúa Sol

Rúa Maria

Rúa Dolores

Rúa Real >

✉ *Correos*

Av. A Coruña

Av. A Coruña

▪ *Teatro Jofre*

BARRIO MAGDALENA

✝ ❺ *Concatedral de San Xiao*
Credencial / Sello

Rúa Sánchez Barcáiziegui

Rúa Igrexa

Suizo Ⓗ

Bla Bla

Rúa Méndez Núñez

Plaza Amboage

Rúa Sol

Rúa Magdalena

O' Xantar Ⓗ

Rúa S.Diego

Rúa Igrexa

Rúa Maria

Plaza Pondal

r/ dos Irmandinos

NAVAL BASE

Rúa Alegre

N

FERROL

Ⓗ

Parador

Fuente de San Roque ❹

❸ ✝ *San Francisco*
(Jardines Herrera)

Pizzaria Ⓗ

Bodegón Ⓗ

Rúa Estrela

Frank

c/ S. Francisco

Parque Raiña Sofia

r/Rastro

Av. Breogán

Rúa Espartero

Ⓐ **Alb.Ferrol**

Camiño do Inglés Ⓗ

Estrada Alta

Via Compostellam

N.S. Socorro

❼ ⓘ *La Gruta*

Paseo Marina

La Cortina

Punto de Partida
First waymark / mojón / monolito

CAMINO GUIDES.COM

Baluarte De San Xoán ❷

Estrada Porto Graña

Jardin de la Ranita

1 FERROL – NEDA

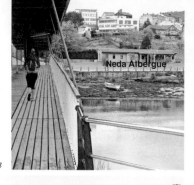

Neda Albergue

⋯⋯⋯	--- ---	8.0	--- ---	55%
	--- ---	5.2	--- ---	28%
	--- ---	<u>1.2</u>	--- ---	8%
Total km		**14.4** km	*(8.9 ml)*

Total ascent **590**m ±**1** *hr**

Alto.m ▲ Couto **70** m (230 ft)

< Ⓐ Ⓗ > ➲ Gándara: **7.0** km+*200m*

100m
FERROL ⋯⋯⋯⋯⋯⋯⋯⋯ S.Maria ⋯⋯ 70m▲ M°Xubia ⋯⋯⋯⋯ **NEDA**
†Pasarela Ⓐ
0 km — Ría de Ferrol — 5 km N-13 [Fene] — Ferrocarril — Ría de Ferrol — 10 km — 15

The Practical Path: The first stage to Neda is alongside the dramatic Ría Ferrol with a mix of city pavements, quiet country lanes and over half is along woodland paths. *(*Allow ±3½ hours to walk 14.4 km at average pace of 4 kph [14.4 ÷4] +55 mins for cumulative ascent of 550m = 4½ hours total. See p17).* There are several hotels in Neda / Xubia and the pilgrim hostel is well located on the estuary where the Río Xubia meets the Ría Ferrol. Alternative routes can be taken from **Ferrol direct to Pontedeume:** ❶ ● via the busy road bridge FE–14 (**19.4** km). ❷ ● via a dramatic pedestrian walkway *pasarela / ferrocarril* alongside the railway (**23.9** km). *(Allow ±6 hrs to walk 23.9 km +2¼ hrs for combined ascent of 1,400m = 8¼ hrs total. See next stage).*

The Mystical Path: *I felt once more how simple and frugal a thing is happiness: a glass of wine... the sound of the sea.* Zorba the Greek.
How natural is the way of the pilgrim: a simple meal, a bed for the night... but it is easy to get distracted in the busyness of the city. We enjoyed and celebrated the act of simplifying in preparation for our pilgrimage. Yesterday life felt so full and our needs so great. Today our goal is simple - we look for the path, shelter, sustenance and carry all that we need on our backs.

0.0 km **Punto de Partida** A Stone plinth (photo>) marks the starting point of the *camino Inglés* adj. the pilgrim information centre *Via Compostellam*. Proceed under archway & follow waymarks through town passing neoclassical **Igrexa de San Francisco** (right)up past **Fuente de San Roque**(left). Keep s/o via Rúa Real and down right> (imm. after statue of cloaked figure with conical hat *capirote)* into Rúa Terra. Cross park onto main road that skirts the coast but is separated from the sea by military zone *Zonar Militar*. Follow around the estuary until we reach a major roundabout.

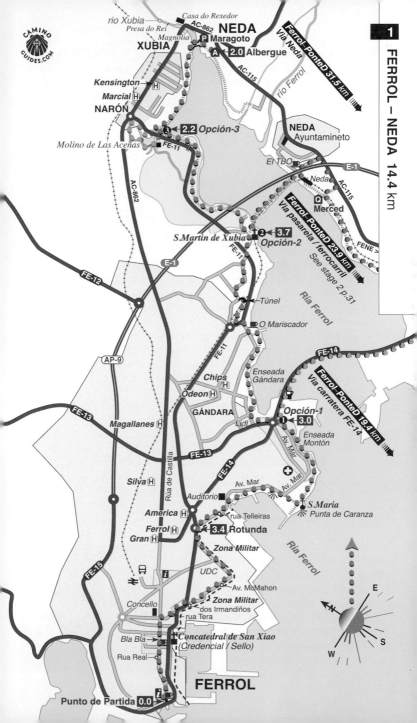

CAMINO GUIDES.COM

rio Xubia
Presa do Rei
Magnolia
AC-862
Casa do Rexedor
NEDA

XUBIA
P
Maragoto
A ◄ **2.0** **Albergue**

Via Neda

Ferrol – PonteD 31.5 km

AC-115

rio Ferrol

Kensington
H
Marcial
H
NARÓN

NEDA
Ayuntamineto

❸ **2.2** *Opción-3*

Molino de Las Aceñas
FE-11

EI TBO
E-1

Neda
AC-115
Q
Merced

Via pasarela /terrocarril

Ferrol PonteD 23.9 km

FENE ►

S.Martin de Xubia
FE-11
❷ **3.7**
Opción-2

See stage 2 p.31

E-1

Túnel

O Mariscador

Ria Ferrol

AP-9

FE-11

Chips
H
Odeon H
GÁNDARA

Enseada
Gándara

FE-14

Ferrol PonteD 19.4 km

FE-12

Magallanes H

Lidl
❶ **3.0**
Opción-1

Via carretera FE-14

FE-13

Enseada
Montón

FE-13

FE-14

Av. Mar

Silva H

Av. Mar
Av. Mar

Auditorio

✚

America H
Ferrol H
Gran H

rua Telleiras

3.4 **Rotunda**

✝ **S.Maria**
✞ **Punta de Caranza**

Zona Militar

Ria Ferrol

FE-15

🚉
ℹ
🚊

UDC
Av. McMahon

Zona Militar
dos Irmandiños
rua Tera

Concello

Bla Bla
✝ **Concatedral de San Xiao**
(*Credencial / Sello*)

Rua Real

ℹ

FERROL

Punto de Partida **0.0**

E
N
S
W

3.4 km **Rotunda** Turn right and right again onto **path** [**0.5** km] around sandy bay into Av. del Mar with fine views of the estuary. At the end of the avenue we reach Caranza beach and **capela Santa Maria** [**1.3** km] and continue around the bay keeping to the pathway with water fonts [🚰] before rejoining Av. del Mar just before **roundabout** [**1.2** km].

3.0 km **Rotunda** *Opción* ❶ ▲▼ continue s/o (straight on) for main waymarked route or turn up right direct to Pontedeume as follows:

Opción ❶ ●●● **Ferrol** to **Pontedeume** direct by road bridge **19.4** km -v- **31.5** km via Neda. This route is all by busy main road (footpath). ▼ At roundabout turn up right to take the main road bridge over the wide estuary. Rejoin waymarked route in **Fene** where it crosses the N-651 onto Av. Concello with two pilgrim friendly cafés at this junction.

▲ For main route keep s/o *under* motorway. Take next right to enter an industrial estate *Polígono* between Ferrol and Narón with several modern hotels. ***Polígono da Gándara:*** •*H·* **Chips** *x11* €35+ ⓒ 981801295 +🍴 Av. Mar 96. •*H····*****Sercotel Odeón** *x85* €45-50 ⓒ 981 372 951 c/Castelao 17. •*P* **Casa Juanito** *x40* €30+ ⓒ 981 388 454 ctra/Concepción Arenal 163. Take path skirting edge of the estuary then rejoin road passing 🚰/🍴 *O Mariscador* to busy roundabout. Cross motorway via bridge and turn down right> to take path along railway line. Emerge in a suburban area to follow waymarks along quiet roads to Igrexa y Monasterio de San Martin de Xubia (photo opp).

3.7 km **Monasterio** *Opción* ❷ *San Martiño de Xubia* ▲▼ Main route s/o.

Option ❷ ●●● **Ferrol** to **Pontedeume 23.9** km -v- **31.5** km via Neda. By Pasarela alongside railway viaduct, missing the quiet pathways into and out of Neda. ▼At *Monasterio de San Martiño* turn down right and take path <left onto footpath alongside railway bridge set high above the estuary with dramatic views (see photo opposite). At far side turn left under AP-9 motorway to pick up waymarks again and rejoin main route or take second alt. green route to Fene (see next stage).

The monastery (also known as O Couto) was first documented in 977 and was transferred to the Cluniac order in 1113. The current Romanesque building dates from the beginning of the XIIth century. The apse to the rear has finely carved corbels showing animal motifs and scenes of erotica. It was the main historic starting point for the pilgrimage to *San Andrés de Teixido*

and continues to provide a waymarked camino to the shrine of St. Andrew; a distance of around 39 km (see page 9 for more details).

▲ Keep s/o up past cruceiro and turn right onto a lane with fine views over the estuary onto earth track through eucalyptus forest. Continue along path which runs parallel to the main road (FE-11) until we reach a bridge over the ria and option point:

2.2 km   Puente *Opción* ❸ **Muíño das Aceas** *Molino de Las Aceñas* ▲▼

Option ❸ ● ● ● path over sluice gates 2.8 km -v- **2.0** km **direct** to Neda. ▼ For alt. route turn down right and imm. left under road bridge and up and around the 18th century mill which was powered by trapping water at high tide and opening the sluice gates at low water to drive the mill wheels. Site of Roman salt mines.

▲ For direct route keep s/o over estuary bridge drop down to take the delightful marine paseo alongside the sea wall. *[if you detour left 50m **under** the bridge at this point there is a good view over the mill race and sluice gates described above which joins here]*. Continue through extensive parkland alongside the estuary with water fonts and rest areas. Just past the *Parque Canino* [**Detour Narón / Xubia**: *town centre for supermercado, restaurants and •H̄ **Marcial** x25 €25-33 © 981 384 417 www.hotelmarcial.com r/Río Pereiro 6-8 +400m and •H̄ **Kensington** x27 €24-34 © 981 387 326 Av de Castilla 832 +300m]*. Continue to far end of the park and take the footbridge *pasarela* over the Río Xubia to:

2.1 km   **Santa María de Neda** *opción* stay in the albergue or other accommodation in the area (see next page) or continue towards Pontedeume (see stage2).

San Martin de Xubia

Opción 2 >>>

●*Albergue* **Neda** *Xunta.[26÷2]* €10
ⓒ659 684 435 / ⓒ 682 623 335
Paseo de Ría Ferrol (O' Empedrón).
Situated on a lovely parkland
site overlooking the estuary. The
purpose-built albergue offers all
modern facilities. Extensive parkland
surrounds the hostel with frontage to
the river esturary and picnic tables for
dining *al fresco*.

Other lodging nearby: In addition to
the hotels and various restaurants in
Narón (see previous page) is 300m
detour to popular •*P'***Maragoto**
€21– €39 ⓒ 981 347 538 *www.
pensionmaragoto.com* Av. Xubia, 12
(AC-115) with bar/🍴. Opp. 🍴 *La
Flor de Mayo* & 🍴 *Mesón Ourra*. Adj.
Xuvia bridge (medieval elements) is
the old mint building *Casa do Rexedor*

built in 1790 originally to supply sheet copper to othe shipyards in Ferrol. in
1811 it commenced minting copper coins under Fernando VII.

The King's Dam *Presa do Rei* upstream
provided the power (see photo). On
the far side of the road bridge between
Xubia and Narón at the top (narrow)
end of the estuary we find the ancient
Queen's Magnolia *Magnolio de la
Reina* thought to be around 300 years
old and reptuedly brought back by a
trader from the Phillipine Islands.

Reflections:

"I am doing the camino once again, looking for something I left behind or perhaps never found. It's like coming home."

_____
_____
_____
_____
_____
_____
_____
_____
_____
_____
_____
_____
_____
_____
_____
_____
_____
_____
_____
_____
_____
_____
_____
_____
_____
_____
_____
_____
_____
_____
_____
_____
_____
_____
_____

2 NEDA – PONTEDEUME

Santiago – 102.7 km *(63.8 ml)*

....	--- ---	4.1	--- ---	31%
———	--- ---	9.5	--- ---	69%
▬▬▬	--- ---	<u>1.1</u>	--- ---	0%
Total km	--- ---	**14.7** km	*(9.2 ml)*	

Total ascent **810**m **±1½** *hr*

Alto.*m* ▲ Vilar do Colo **205**m *(672 ft)*

< Ⓐ Ⓗ > ❯Vilar do colo **10.4** km ❯Cabanas **13.6** km.

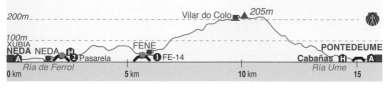

The Practical Path: This stage brings with it our first big climb, up to **Vilar do Colo.** While it is relatively challenging (particularly for those who have joined together stages 1 and 2) we are rewarded with fine views and there are an increasing number of rest stops offering refreshment. Despite this it is wise to take advantage of the good facilities in **Fene** and ensure our water bottles are topped up whenever possible. The majority of this stage is on tarmac, so greener alternatives have been offered where possible. Almost as challenging as the climb is the sharp decent into **Cabañas** and the attractive riverside town of **Pontedeume** where this stage ends.

The Mystical Path: *You are the sky. Everything else; it's just the weather.*

Pema Chödrön.

The camino both delights and challenge us. The highs and lows mirroring life's ups and down. But, despite our outer circumstances, the clear blue sky is always there... above the clouds. Perhaps it is this place of peace we are struggling to find, not realising it was there all along.

0.0 km **Neda Albergue** Leave the hostel and follow the estuary south along coastal paths and boardwalks and cross the Río Belelle *[which powered the many mills that ground the wheat for the Bread of Neda famous as far back as 1590 when its 'sea bread' fed the Spanish navy and the armada!].* We rejoin the road to enter the village of **Neda** at *Igrexa de Santa María* with plaque placed by the UK Confraternity of St James commemorating the 2004 Holy Year. *[The church contains an unusual 16th century image of Christ with chain* **Cristo da Cadea** *brought here from England. There is a recurring theme in Galicia of images of Christ appearing from the sea and returning whence they came. Hence the chain to prevent the image from departing!].*

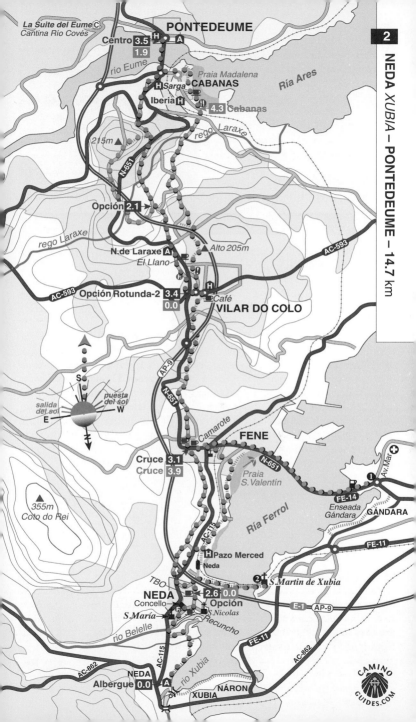

PONTEDEUME

La Suite del Eume C.
Cantina Río Covés

Centro **3.5**
1.9

río Eume

Praia Madalena

H *Sarga*
Iberia H
CABANAS
4.3 Cabanas

rego Laraxe

Ría Ares

▲ 215m

N-651

Opción **2.1**

rego Laraxe

▲ Alto 205m

N. de Laraxe A
El Llano

AC-593

AC-593

Opción Rotunda-2 **3.4**
0.0

Café
H
VILAR DO COLO

AP-9

N-651

N
S
puesta del sol
salida del sol
E
W

Camarote

FENE

Cruce **3.1**
Cruce **3.9**

Praia S.Valentín

N-651

❶
Av.Mar
FE-14
Enseada Gándara
GÁNDARA

AC-115

Ría Ferrol

FE-11

▲ 355m
Coto do Rei

H *Pazo Merced*
Neda

❷
S.Martín de Xubia

E-1 AP-9

TBO

2.6 **0.0**

NEDA
Concello
S.María
S Nicolas
Opción
Recuncho

río Belelle

FE-11

AC-862

NEDA
Albergue **0.0**

A

río Xubia

XUBIA **NÁRON**

AC-115

AC-862

CAMINO
GUIDES.COM

Continue to the rear of the church by playground [🚰] cross pedestrian bridge *pasarela* and past the Council offices **Concello** with pilgrim stamp *sello* [🚰]. [🍴/ *bakery on main road 100m*]. Keep s/o to welcome shop and bar *Tienda y Taberna O Recuncho*. 50m beyond option. ◆

[**Detour** *100m (right–no sign)*
Rua do Castro to 14th century **Igrexa San Nicolás** and stone cross **cruceiro** (photo above) with lovely views to the rear over the mouth of the río Belelle and ría Ferrol].

◆ The route continues left into modern suburbs passing *Meson O Fumazo* (left 50m) to option point:

2.6 km **Opción** ▲▼ 🍴 *El TBO* The waymarked route turns left, under the AP-9, uphill to cross busy main road [!] then climb steeply inland before dropping down again into Fene - all by asphalt. There is an option to continue parallel to the coast to rejoin the waymarked route in Fene:

▲ **Alternative coastal path** to Fene **3.9** km -v- **3.1** km. Keep s/o past 🍴 *El TBO* to AP-9 flyover where alternative route ❷ from *San Martín de Xubia* joins. With no official pedestrian crossing at **Neda rail station** we follow the waymarked route up to cross main road AC-115. Here alt. route **turns right>** under AP-9 to follow main road for 50m then turn right> signposted **Pazo Merced [0.9** km]. Follow lane down to cross railway via bridge at •*H*˙˙˙**Pazo da Merced** *x8* €100+ ✆ 981 382 200 *www.pazodamerced.com* luxury hotel directly on Ría Ferrol, garden bar generally open to non-residents.

Turn <left to take the path alongside railway to emerge on lane at **boat pier [0.7** km] continue onto lane parallel to railway to join Rúa Camiño Regueiro at sign Concello de Fene. In 50m take track right> (house Nº 35) onto **boardwalks [0.6** km] onto Playa De San Valentín. Turn <left to cross the park (passing sports ground) continue up Av. Mar, and follow the road to the right before turning left through **rail underpass [1.0** km]. Just *before* **road underpass [0.1** km] turn up steps left *this* side of the N-651 by cemetery and onto main road. Veer left to pass Igrexa San Salvador and keep s/o along main road to join waymarked route at 🍴 *O Camarote* **[0.6** km] – **Total 3.9** km.

▲ To continue on newly waymarked route turn left at option point, under flyover and up to cross over AC-115 by junction of the AP-9 motorway. Follow waymark ahead pointing us uphill on minor road then veer right to cross over the motorway. Continue along the road to crest of the hill were we are rewarded with views of the Ría Ferrol [**1.2** km]. Follow ample waymarks along the road down into Fene [**1.9** km].

3.1 km **Cruce *Fene*** Cross main road (N-651) in centre of town with several cafés incl. 🍴 *O Camarote* & 🍴 *Lembranza* on main road (alt. coast route joins from right). Good place to take a rest before the steep climb up to Vilar do Coto. *[+1.1 km •P¨A Cepa x8* €25-40 Ⓒ *981 341 352 c/Hortela 16].* Continue past 🍴 *A Ponte* out of town to **lavanderia** [⌂] [**1.2** km] and adj. mill. Up steeply onto path through woodland under the AP-9 and up to Gadis supermarket and industrial estate at roundabout in **Vilar do Coto** [**2.2** km].

3.4 km **Rotunda *Vila do Colo*** (with 🍴 *Vila do Colo* and •H¨*Chips x36* €70+). Turn left at *Gadis* roundabout and at *next* **roundabout** [**0.1** km] is *Option* ◆◆ The authorities have re-waymarked the route along the busy N-651 with several crossings. For this newly waymarked route keep s/o *under* road bridge visible ahead.

◆ **Original route** to **Pontedeume 6.3***km* -v- **5.6***km.* **NB:** This follows a delightful series of forest tracks and quiet country lanes to the beach at Cabanas by Pontedeume. The original waymarks are fading fast and have been erased at the start but recommence shortly afterwards. ◆ Turn right at roundabout (sign Pontedeume) and turn right> again 50m *before* the crash barriers **onto path** [**0.3** km] depending on time of year it may be necessary to push through the undergrowth (only 200m!) then s/o over side road onto path through woodland to cross the **AP-9 motorway** [**1.3** km]. Turn <left and next right> down woodland path to emerge on series of lanes and where the Camiño de Val Dabaixo joins Rúa do Batán turn left and at the bottom keep s/o to join wet path by **río de Laraxe** [**2.2** km] and turn left up to join road down to cross over the **AC-122** [**0.6** km] and take the steps opposite down under railway into **Cabañas** *[Hotels see main route for details].*

Take the first right (opp. gym Hammer Strength) to **Cabanas playa** [**0.4** km] (visible ahead) and 🍴 *O' Chiringuito.*

Beach bars and restaurants line the delightful beach or take the parallel path through the pine trees to red & white harbour beacon and take the boardwalk to 1st roundabout (hotels left) s/o to **2nd roundabout** [**1.1** km] where the main route joins and continue over the Ponte de Eume to 3rd roundabout in the centre of **Pontedeume** [**0.6** km] **–Total 6.3** km.

◆ For the waymarked route in **Vila do Colo** at the option point continue s/o under the road bridge and take the steps on the far side up to the N-651 [**!**]. Shortly after turn <left then right> onto quiet road, pass [⌂] and sign for 🍴 *El Llano* before rejoining main road past ●*Alb*. **Natureza de Laraxe** *Priv. [16÷1]* €19 +4 €70 ℂ 981 430 270. Turn right> down short, steep track then <left down country road, under AP-9 motorway, and follow to option:

2.1 km **Opción ▲▼** Here we are presented with an illogical alternative as it has no historical or practical basis. It doubles the distance (**2.6 km** -v- **1.2** km) and doubles the height climbed (**215**m -v- **105**m)!

▼ To take this 'complementario' route turn left back up and under the AP-9 over the rego de Laraxe and up steeply to cross over the AP-9 to high point 215m with good views over the ría Ares. Then back down again through a short stretch of woodland to rejoin the main route near the N-651 (see map).

▲ To continue on the main route turn right at option point over *rego de Laraxe* and crossover N-651[**!**] back down to join the AC-141 [⌂] (left) and veer left onto parallel secondary road to re-emerge at 🍴 *Fragas de Eume* and ●*H*˙˙˙**Sarga** *x80* €43-55 ℂ 981 431 000 c/ Arenal 7. (+ 400m ●*H*˙**Iberia** *x76* €32-40 ℂ 607 451 010 Paseo Magdalena 32 - summer only). Continue s/o over roundabout to cross the 16th century bridge that once boasted an impressive 79 arches as well as a chapel. While only 15 arches remain today the bridge remains an impressive sight and fine entry over the Río Eume into **Pontedeume** town.

3.5 km **Pontedeume** *Centro*. A delightful town full of activity (especially in the summer tourist season). To go direct to the municipal albergue turn right along the riverbank for 200m. To access the historic town *ciudad vieja* continue over roundabout into Rua Real along waymarked camino. Numerous *restaurants, cafés and bars* 🍴/🍴 spread out along the estuary and line the narrow medieval laneways and squares in the old town where there is choice of alternative accommodation. The tourist office is situated in the old tower ❶*Torreón dos Andrade* (see photo) overlooking the river and set in peaceful gardens just behind the pilgrim hostel. This tower once formed part of the 15th Century Pazo do Conde. In the centre of town verlooking Praza Real is the handsome granite **Concello**.

At the top of town (slightly off the caminos route) is the Gothic **Igrexa de Santiago**. Visit for a quiet reflection or join the 20.00 mass. More details and confirmation of opening times can be found at the tourist office. The facade features a raised relief of Santiago Matamoros while the interior also hosts a graphic statue of Santiago Matamoros (photo>). Like so many of the town's other landmarks it was commissioned by Fernán Pérez de Andrade (in 1538) and a marble statue in his honour can also be found inside. Alterations were commissioned to the facade in the 1700's by Bartolomé Rajoy (Archbishop of Santiago) in classic baroque style.

Pontedeume: ❶ *Turismo* Torreón de Los Andrade 10.30–14.00 & 16.00–19.00. Festivos 11.00–14.00. Adj. the rear steps by the fountain, overlooking the estuary is ¶ *O' Trasteir*

•*Lodging:*❶*Alb.* **Pontedeume** *Muni.* *[10÷1]* €10 ⓒ 981 430 270 c/ del Muelle (see photo>). ❷ *H***Eumesa** *x60* €40-65 ⓒ 981 430 901 *www.hoteleumesa.es* Av. La Coruña (rotunda).❸*Alb.* **Río Eume** *Priv.* *[20÷3]* €17 ⓒ 604 036 109 *www.alberguerioeume.es* r/Club Firrete *19* *(+500m).* ❹*Hs¨***Allegue** *x6* €30-40

ⓒ981 430 035 c/Chafaris 1. ❺*P˙***Luís** *x4* €18-€36 ⓒ 981 430 235 c/San Agustín 12. ❻*P¨***A Falúa***x8* €69 ⓒ 881 291 861 r/Ferreiros, 25. ❼*Hs˙* **Norte** €30 ⓒ 981 434 527 c/ San Agustín 26. ❽*P* **Casa Apilladeira** *x4* €45+ ⓒ 638 962 554 r/Pescadería 19. •*Lodging Suburbs (exit):* ❾*H.***Montebreamo** *x6* €50-70 ⓒ600 327 230 *www.hmontebreamo.es* top of town on main road N-VI c/Barro 38 *+1.1* km from town centre *+100*m off route]. ❿*P* **Mesón Paz** *x5* €30-40 ⓒ 981 432 024 *www.pensionmesonpaz.com* c/Campolongo 92 *+250*m off route. *CR* **Eume** *x4* ⓒ 981 434 057 *+1.2* km off route. Note also hotels in *Cabanas* on the other side of the bridge.

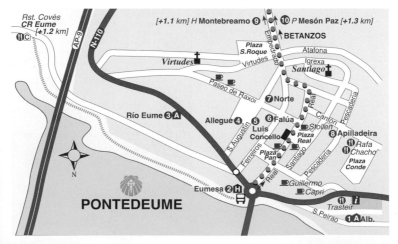

Igrexa de Santiago

Reflections:

_____
_____
_____
_____
_____
_____
_____
_____
_____
_____
_____
_____
_____
_____
_____
_____
_____
_____
_____
_____
_____
_____
_____
_____
_____
_____

Pilgrims near the Albergue in Pontedeume overlooking the río Eume.

3 PONTEDEUME – BETANZOS

Santiago – 88.0 km *(54.7 ml)*

|||||||||||	--- ---	5.4	--- ---	26%
▬▬▬	--- ---	15.5	--- ---	74%
▬▬▬	--- ---	0.0	--- ---	0%
Total km		**20.9** km *(123.0 ml)*		

Total ascent **680**m ±1¼ *hr*
Alto.m ▲ Aldea Buiña **180**m *(590 ft)*
< Ⓐ Ⓗ > ➲ Miño: **10.3** km

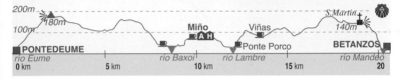

The Practical Path: This stage begins with a very steep climb out of Pontedeume but the effort is rewarded with fine views and tranquil woodland paths. The route takes us through Miño with good facilities and pilgrim hostel for those wishing to break this stage at the halfway point. There is a small beach and café at Ponte do Porco to refresh before another climb to San Martin and then finally descend sharply into the enchanting medieval town of Betanzos.

The Mystical Path: *No man ever steps in the same river twice for it is not the same river and He is not the same man. Heraclitus.*
Who am I now and who do I wish to be when I reach the end of this journey? As I begin to surrender and allow the camino to strip away all that is superflous what will I find of my Self underneath?

0.0 km **Pontedeume** *Centro* From the roundabout take Rúa Real up through the town centre passing *Concello (left)* on Praza Real up through Prazas Angustias *Igrexa Santiago (right 50m)* and Plaza San Roque. Continue up steeply [**1.0** km]. *[● **Detour** right **3.0** km by road I**grexa San Miguel de Breamo** built 1187 as an Augustinian monastery – see photo>. A local pilgrimage takes place in May & September].* At the top  of this very steep climb *Casa Cermuzo Alto. 180m* fine views and secondary access to S.Miguel de Breamo. Continue to pass [⛲] *Lavadero-fuente-merendero* **Buiña** [**1.7** km]

CAMINO
GUIDES.COM

BETANZOS

H i 🏛️
A **2.0** Centro

AP-9 E-1

175m
Iglesia St Martin 3.9 🏛️
S.Piao
Betanzos Vello

F

N-651

Hosteleria
Fonte de Gas F

Refrescos
Chantada

F
Parque
Garea

Sas

Viñas 2.8 ⊙ *Navedo*

San Panaleon das Viñas

Ponte Lambre
Rio Lambre

P *Brisa [+800m]*
Praia

Ponte do Porco 1.8 F

H 🏛️ **2.1** Miño
f
A H

AC-160

Ponte Baxoi 3.6 ◼
Ultreia y Suseia

⊙ *Rio de Bembre*

rio Baxoi

AP-9 E-1

rio Xario

4.6 Campo de Golf

F ✕

S

puesta
del sol W

F ✕

E
salida
del sol

N-651

🏛️ *S. Miguel de Breamo*

⊙ *Ventosa*

180m
Montebreamo H *Alto*

PONTEDEUME

C

H A
Eumesa **0.0** Centro

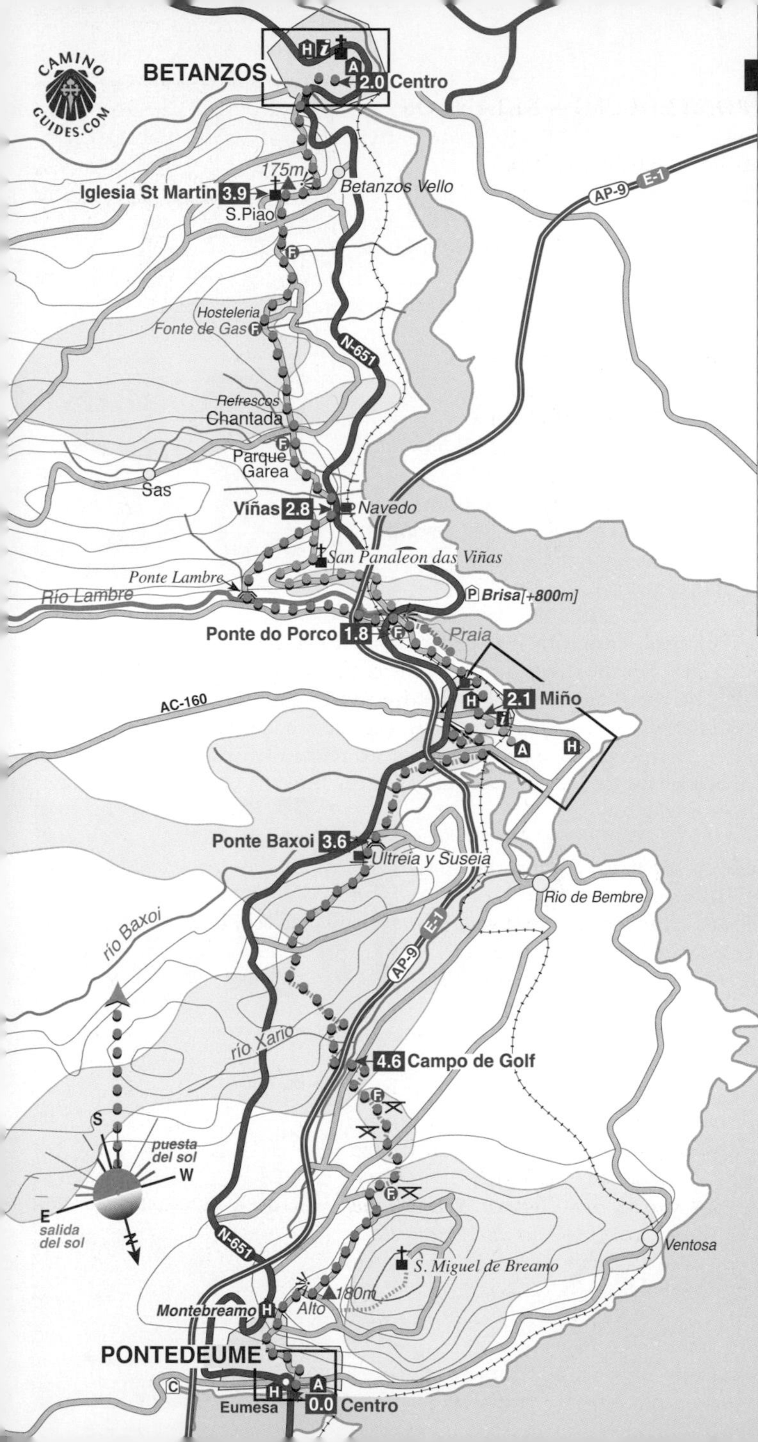

and turn right to pass through an arch of grapevines onto an earth path past another picnic area [🏕] to cross road onto **Club Golf de Miño [1.9 km].**

4.6 km **Campo de Golf** Continue along the well maintained footpath over pasarela río Viadeiro and over the AP-9 motorway and past Cultural Viadeiro down steeply to Ponte Baxoi and welcome 🍴. *[Historically the steep descent and high banks here were infamous for stagecoach robberies. And in 1809 this was the site of fierce battles between Napoleonic troops and Galician guerrilla fighters].*

3.6 km **Ponte Baxoi** 🍴*Ultreia y Suseia* novel cafe built into a woodworking factory. Just beyond is the Ponte Baxoi one of several bridges built under the aegis of Fernán Pérez de Andrade 'The Good' at the end of the 14th century (We pass another gem on this stage at Lambre also from the same epoch and patronage). We now

continue by level earth path between the río Baxoi and the N-651 and under several flyovers of the AP-9 into the outskirts of Miño along camiño Fonte.

2.1 km **Miño** *Plaza* [🏕] (left) 🍴 *Green* (right) by Concello. Bustling town with good facilities incl. ❶ Tourist office (summer) and several popular beaches including *Praia Grande* extending to over 1 kilometre of sand and located only 500m beyond the municipal albergue .

●**Miño** *Detour*: ●*Alb.* Miño *Muni.* *[22÷2]* €10 ℂ 689 233 678 Rúa Marismas. *Directions*: Veer right onto Rúa Pardineira then right> on main road past Turismo and over railway. Take 3rd turning right> into r/ Marismas and follow this all the way down to the end and <left to hostel.

Also off route overlooking *Praia Grande* •*P* **O Cantiño** €25 © 981 782 007 r/ Loyos & •*H* **Crisol de las Rías** *x24* €35-45 © 981 778 895.

To continue to Betanzos leave town via r/Barrosa passing ⛟ *A Buchaca,* ⛟ *Vidal* and ⛟ *15 Once'* with terrace overlooking estuary. •*Hs*¨**La Terraza** *x20* €35-45 © 657 629 292 *www.hlaterraza.com* r/A Carreira 4 adj. ⛟ *Sophia* and veer right over rail via footbridge. Continue along quiet country lanes to Ponte do Porco. *(Note:* ● *A short alt. route into Ponte do Porco, parallel to the road, via boardwalk along river estuary is clearly visible on our right).*

1.8 km **Ponte do Porco** With closed ⛟ by small shaded square [⛲] overlooking estuary. *(◆Note: the original route crossed over the river here and up steep country roads through pine woods into Montecelo & Paderne **Igrexa San Pantaleon das Viñas** XIII to join the new route to enter Viñas on N-651).* *(+800m •P **Brisa** x10 €40 © 981 782 022, Aldea Insua).*

◆The main waymarked route now takes a more pleasant course continuing s/o *this* side of the road bridge under AP-9 flyover alongside río Lambre. Turn right over the river via the emblematic medieval Ponte Lambre (see photo top of stage 3). *[Site of the romantic legend of the servant Roxín Roxal who fell in love with his masters daughter Teresa. Roxín was exiled and Teresa betrothed to the knight Henrique. To prove his valour Henrique fought a wild boar on the bridge but only wounded the beast who then killed Teresa. Some days later the body of the boar was found on the bridge killed with a dagger that had been gifted to Roxín by Teresa's father!].* Proceed over the bridge into woodland and up steeply before dropping down into Viñas on the main N-651:

2.8 km **Viñas** *N-651* ⛟ *Nevado* Turn left along main road and left again after 100m. Continue along quiet roads past Chantada 'cultural park' Parque Garea, continue past hilltop donativo pilgrim rest area then over rego da fonte past *fuente Cinos Dela* [⛲] & *Fonte de gas [sign for Hostalería right – no information].* We now follow this high contour with views over the river estuary passing [⛲] down steps (right) below the road and shaded picnic area at S.Paio A Rua before reaching a high point at 140m at the church of saint Martin of Tiobre with fine views overlooking Betanzos and the river estuary.

3.9 km **Igrexa** *San Martiño de Tiobre* Beautiful 12[th]century romanesque church with exquisite corbels, tympanus and  motifs. *[400m down to the right of the crossroads (off route) is Betanzos O Vello which is thought to be the pre-roman Celtic origins of present day Betanzos. Built on high ground away from maurading sea pirates].* We now follow the country road steeply downhill to the suburbs above **Betanzos** by the church of Nsa. Sra.

do Camiño with cruceiro and [⛲] before crossing the handsome medieval bridge *Puente Viejo* over the Río Mandeo. Here on 18th & 26th August is the colourful river boat festival *Gira a los Caneiros*. We enter **Betanzos** through an arched gate (see photo >) and follow the cobbled lane up into the town. At the crossroads with Rúa Castro there is a choice to turn right to go direct to the municipal albergue or left into the central square and alternative accommodation.

2.1 km **Betanzos** *Centro* known as *Flavium Brigantium* in Roman times and retaining many historic buildings off its bustling central square *Praza Irmáns García Naveira (Praza Galicia or praza do Campo)* with handsome fountain and statue of Diana *Fonte de Diana Cazadora (see photo next page)*. The town makes an ideal pilgrim halt with variety of lodging, bars and restaurants around the central

square or down by the river. A former fishing centre and trade hub **Betanzos** was the capital of one of Galicia's 7 provinces in the 16th century. Despite developments over the centuries the town's ancient walls still remain with 3 of the original entrance gates.

The municipal albergue pays a respectful nod to the towns fishing past with plaque displaying the original name 'House of the Fishmonger' *Casa da Pescadaria*. Recently refurbished with good facilities (incl. modern kitchen) yet retaining the buildings original character and charm.

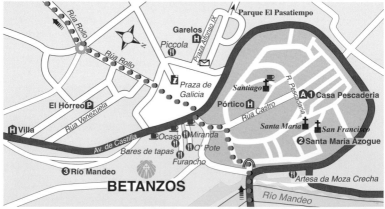

BETANZOS

Nearby is *Igrexa de Santa María do Azougue* XV & cruceiro adj. *Igrexa San Francisco* XIV which houses the tombs of prominent Galician noblemen, including Fernán Pérez de Andrade "O Boo" who commissioned the buildings

around this square named after him. This is a quiet area of town away from the main activity, offering space for quiet reflection. Also in the old town is the impressive *Igrexa de Santiago* XV (fine west door see photo>) opp. ☕ *Lanzos* popular with locals who congregate here for the homemade cakes. Back down rua Castro is ☕ *Banca* overlooking Praza Constitution.

We can stay in the quiet streets of the old town or join the action and explore the alleyways off the modern central square which are filled with *tapas bars* 🍴 and a lively atmosphere. The festival of pilgrim saint San Roque is celebrated here on the 16th August when a giant balloon is set alight and launched from the tower of the church of San Domingos adj. the statue of huntress Diana. If you have time to explore there is also a Victorian theme park *Parque El Pasatiempo* on the outskirts of town,

inspired and created by two locals who had made their fortune in the New World and on returning to Galicia wanted to share some of the interesting developments they had seen there.

❶ Betanzos: *Turismo* 10.00 –14.00 / 17.00–20.00 Praza de Galicia. *Albergues:* ❶ Betanzos *Muni.[35÷3]* €10 *Casa da Pescaderia* r/Pescadaria (see photo>). ❷ **Santa María del Azogue** *Asoc.[16÷2]* €12 ✆ 981 819 635 r/Santa María (corner). ❸ **Río Mandeo** *Asoc.[24÷3]* €17 +3 €70 ✆ 604 044 448 r/Doctor Fleming, 3.

Hotels: •*Hs* **Pórtico** *x14* €55-75 ✆ 981 458 818 *www.hostalportico.com* r/ Castro 8. •*Hs"* **Garelos** *x22* €50-75 ✆ 981 775 930 *www.hotelgarelos.com* c/ Alfonso IX, 8. •*P"* **El Hórreo** *x5* €15-€30 ✆ 669 191 387 c/ Venezuela 26. Top of town and price bracket: •*H"'* **Villa** *Palacete x30* €51-66 ✆ 981 776 682 *www.hotelvilladebetanzos.com* Av. de Castilla 38.

Reflections:

_____
_____
_____
_____
_____
_____
_____
_____
_____
_____
_____
_____
_____
_____
_____
_____
_____
_____
_____
_____
_____
_____
_____
_____
_____
_____
_____
_____
_____
_____
_____
_____
_____

Igrexa Santa Maria XV with the cruceiro de Santa María (foreground) adjacent to th Igrexa San Francisco XIV.

4 BETANZOS – BRUMA

Santiago 67.1 km *(41.7 ml)*

▪▪▪▪▪▪▪▪▪▪ --- ---	12.6 --- ---	50%
━━━━ --- ---	10.9 --- ---	43%
▬▬▬ --- ---	<u>1.6</u> --- ---	7%
Total km	**25.1** km *(15.6 ml)*

▲ Total ascent **890**m ±**1½** *hr*

Alto.m ▲ As Travesas **490** m *(1,607 ft)*

< Ⓐ Ⓗ > ➲ Presedo **11.9** km ➲ Encorro de Beche **17.2** km

The Practical Path: A demanding stage with a steep climb out of ***Betanzos*** up into ***Hospital de Bruma***. The route has been re-waymarked (the original way is shown in grey) and now 50% is on lovely forest paths but it does now include 1.6 km of the busy AC-542 *[!]*. Facilities along this stage are limited but an albergue and pilgrim café around halfway provides a popular break and option to split the stage at ***Presedo*** or 5km further on at Encorro de Beche. Bruma is a small but delightful hamlet with two albergues and welcoming 🍴/🍽. Alternative lodging in ***Meson do Vento*** 1.9 km off route.

The Mystical Path: *I found my heart upon a mountain I did not know I could climb... Laurel Bleadon Maffei.*
Where is it we fear to go? Are we afraid to go onward or is it possible what we really fear is to go *inward*. The journey ahead is long but only by testing our inner resolve will we discover our real strength – outer and inner.

0.0 km **Betanzos** *Centro* Cross central square and take Rúa Rollo to cross over Rio Mandeo *Ponte de Cascas* before turning up left onto a small country road that winds steeply uphill and out of town. Continue along country roads passing over railway before crossing the **A-6 motorway [2.6** km] Turn imm. right> and then <left to follow lanes to Xanrozo **crossroads [1.0** km] with Concello Requian (right).

3.6 km **Cruce** *Concello* [⛲] picnic area (right). Keep s/o at crossroads. The country lanes are well waymarked but stay focussed on the numerous turnings ahead before taking a stretch of forest path. Rejoin quiet country lane and pass Engas power station (left) and shortly afterwards enter the hamlet of

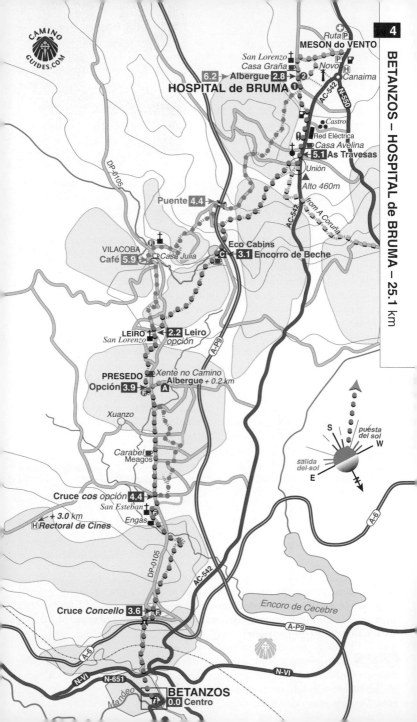

CAMINO GUIDES.COM

Ruta ⓟ
MESÓN do VENTO
San Lorenzo †
Casa Graña 🏠
6.2 ◄ **Albergue** 2.8
HOSPITAL de BRUMA
Novo 🏠
2 🅟 Ⓗ
Ⓟ *Canaima*
AC-542 — N-550

Castro
🚉 Red Eléctrica
† *Casa Avelina*
5.1 **As Travesas**
Unión
▲ *Alto 460m*
from A Coruña
AC-542

Puente 4.4 ►

🏠 **Eco Cabins**
VILACOBA †
Café 5.9 🅕
🏠 *Casa Julia*
Ⓒ 3.1 **Encorro de Beche**

LEIRO †
San Lorenzo
2.2 **Leiro**
opción
A-P9

PRESEDO 🏠 *Xente no Camiño*
Opción 3.9 🅕 Ⓐ **Albergue** + 0.2 km

Xuanzo

Carabel 🏠
Meagos

Cruce *cos* opción 4.4 ►
† *San Esteban* 🅕
+ 3.0 km
Ⓗ *Rectoral de Cines* 🏠 *Engas*

DP-0105
AC-542

Encoro de Cecebre

Cruce *Concello* 3.6 🅕

A-P9

✝ (symbol)

N-VI
N-651
BETANZOS
Mandeo ℹ️ 0.0 **Centro**

N-VI

A-6

S
W
puesta del sol
salida del sol
E

Cos with church of Saint Stephen *Igrexa San Esteban*. Stone cruceiro stands in the square in front of the small parish church. Turn right past *Central Social de Cos* and turn left on main road DP-0105 to crossroads Km-7 and option.

4.4 km **Cruce** *Cos opción* ▲▼ The waymarked route now continues s/o along the busy DP-0105 with poor margins and dangerous bends. There is an option here to ❶ *Detour 3.0 km left* to •*Rectoral de Cines* x10 €70+ © 981 777 710 Casas Novas, Oza dos Ríos, beautifully restored IX century monastic buildings, offers free pick up. Or ❷ *Turn right* to join the original route that runs roughly parallel to the main road through quiet country lanes and forest paths. *Note:* some official waymarks have been removed and others are fading fast so only take this option if you have a good sense of direction!

▼ **Path** to **Presedo 4.0** km *(via forest tracks, poorly waymarked)* -v- **3.9** km *(via busy DP-0105)*. At crossroads (Km-7 sign) turn right and **next left [0.2** km] onto woodland path, keep right on narrow path then turn <left onto country lane to **T-junction [1.2** km]. Turn right and **next left [0.1** km]. Turn right uphill then <left at old waymark in wall. Take next left passing lone house. Keep s/o onto track through woodland at road turn right> then <left onto path, continue in straight direction through series of woodland paths to emerge onto road. Turn <left down road to rejoin waymarked route on main road at **bridge [1.1** km]. Continue into **Presedo [0.6** km] – **Total 4.0** km.

▲ To continue on waymarked road route keep s/o at crossroads past football ground (right) and 🍴*Bar Carabel* [1.1 km] (left) and sign for Igrexa Santiago Meangos (right) to sharp bend in road [**!**] by lavandero (right) to bridge over the **rego de Fontao [2.1** km] (alternative route joins from right). Veer left off main road onto woodland track into **Presedo** [0.7 km].

3.9 km **Presedo** *opción Alb.* ▲▼
At the village entrance we have an option to detour right (200m) ▼ to the main road and cross over into Lugo Campo to ●*Alb.* Presedo *Muni. [16÷1]* €10 © 644 035 292 Campo de La Saletta with all facilities and covered outdoor seating area or...

▲ Keep s/o along path for 400m to welcoming 🍴/🍴 *Xente no Camiño* ©981 673 120 <u>www.mesonmuseo.com</u> look out for signs and gate onto terrace (main entrance on road). Pilgrim theme 🍴/🍴 from artist Alfredo Erias where Maria Teresa offers a range of homemade food and *menú del peregrino* ably assisted by son Pedro.

Keep s/o to join quiet country roads and veer up right by abandoned building onto path and into the village of **Leiro**.

2.2 km **Leiro** *Igrexa* covered seating area adj. parish church of *Santa Eulalia*. *[Note: At the T-junction just beyond the church, waymarks to the original route (left and imm. right s/o – see grey route on map) have been removed here but commence again after a short distance and continue into Vilacoba (Casa Julia). This route avoids the busy AC-542 into Bruma but the newly waymarked route is mostly by delightful forest tracks and woodland paths so this section of the original route is not recommended. It is included to avoid confusion in case you inadvertently stray onto it... or want a change of scene!].*

At the T-junction new waymark up right> and <left on main road [**0.2** km] to veer off right> onto forest track [**0.3** km] through eucalyptus woods to reservoir and picnic area [**2.6** km].

3.1 km **Encorro de Beche Suites Nature** *eco-camp* **cabins** *x6* (sleeps 4 from €100) ✆ 697 894 220 ⬦/⬦ & picnic area by reservoir with toilets/ [⬦]. Continue and turn <left on main road under AP-9 autopista then s/o before we turn up right> onto old road that becomes a forest track.

Follow this uphill and around mink farm. Join quiet country lane to the busy AC-542 [**!**] here alternative route from A Coruña joins from the right at the high point of the camino Inglés *Alto 470m*. We proceed together <left into As Travesas along the main road.

5.1 km **As Travesas** ⬦ *Casa Avelina* Maria Carmen ✆ 981 630 262. *[Pick-up offered from here for guests staying at Hotel Canaima]. Opposite the café is a small chapel dedicated to San Roque – site of local pilgrimage in August.*

We now have a long (1.6 km) slog on the busy AC-542 [**!**] past the *Red Eléctrica de España* at the end of which is a detour down a side road (right) to a Celtic Castro (100m) *Eira dos Mouros* one of the largest castros in Galicia dating back to the 4th century BCE. *[Mouros generally refers to mythical beings who lived underground and often associated with archaeological mounds and the faery folk and **not** with the* Moors of North Africa]. Nothing much remains of the site which was excavated to reveal some Roman artefacts. It is intersected by the Electricity Network substation in an act of unusual cultural barbarism. We pass this side road continuing s/o past Repsol depot (left) and turn

<left by abandoned **Galp station** [**1.6** km] onto track through woodland to join country lane into **Bruma** [**1.2** km]: *[Note: If you are staying in **Meson do Vento** it is possible to continue s/o along the main road by the Galp turn-off but it is recommended to take the safer but longer waymarked route via Bruma].*

2.8 km Hospital de Bruma a peaceful hamlet with ultra modern albergue ❶*Alb.* **San Lorenzo** *Priv.* *[22÷4]* €20 +2 €60 © 619 464 240 <u>www.alberguesanlorenzobruma.com</u> all facilities. In stark contrast to the original medieval pilgrim hostel ❷*Alb.* **Bruma** *Xunta.* *[22÷3]* €10 © 649 580 309 sensitively restored with kitchen

and basic cooking facilities and covered yard for washing and drying clothes, occupying a tranquil riverside site. A welcoming café and restaurant (100m) 🍴/🍴 *Casa Graña* María Graña Bouzas © 981 696 006 *menú peregrino* serves the increasing band of pilgrims that overnight in the area. Adjoining the cafe is the medieval chapel of *San Lorenzo (part dating to XIIc)* which offers mass at 7p.m. on 4th Saturday of each month (check times).

Hospital de Bruma has served as an important junction of the two arms of the Camino Inglés from both Ferrol and A Coruña for many centuries. In the meantime **Meson do Vento** offers beds and also direct bus services to A Coruña for those taking this option (see below).

●●●● **Meson do Vento** [**+1.9** km] Lodging in Bruma is currently limited to the albergues but alternatives are available in Meson do Vento on the AC-542. This can be reached either by turning right *past* San Lorenzo and s/o by country lane. Or turn right imm. *before* the Xunta albergue by playground and take the first forest track <left over stream, veer left again then turn right to follow lane to T-junction where we turn right up to the main road:

◀**Meson do Vento:** Popular (often full) •*P**** **Mesón Novo** *x9* €35-45 ©981 692 776. Opp. •*Apt.* **Fogar do Vento** €60 - 80 (4 places in 2 rooms) © 683 336 918 adj. •*H**** **Canaima** *x18* €44-69 © 981 692 891 (Ramón) <u>www.hotelrestaurantecanaima.com</u> with 🍴 & laundry – adj. garage (shop)

& bus stop. *Detour: 200m South (towards Santiago) along AC-542 into town on Av. Santiago Apóstol 42 [+0.2 km] for ⊕Farmacia and adj 🍴 La Ruta. [Other accommodation accessible by bus or taxi on AC-542 (see map next stage): Castrelos [+4.6 km] •H**Barreiro €35 © 981 680 917. Ordes [+9.3 km] •H**Alda Camiño Inglés x28 €30+ / •Hs**Louro x7 €15+].*

Note: At this juncture there is an opportunity to visit **A Coruña**: A regular bus service stops opposite the *Hotel Canaima*. The hotel keeps a bus schedule (arrives ± every hour, takes ± one hour, costing €3.50). Make sure you alight at the main central bus station on Rua Cabalerios / N-550. The following itinerary makes it possible to incorporate the A Coruña stages adding an extra 2 days as follows:

From **Meson do Vento** take an early morning bus to *A Coruña* central bus station and head north to the old quarter (walk 2.7 km – bus #1 €1 or share a taxi) to the start of the route at the lovely church of Santiago in the historic centre. Explore the old quarter and take the camino out of the city in the afternoon (or stay the night?). Take the alternative (green) coast route to the medieval port of O Burgo and overnight in the Cambre area (± 14 km) and visit the Church of Santa Maria (Jerusalem hydra chalice) the only site in Galicia directly associated with the life of Jesus (see p.68). The following day walk back to Bruma (± 20.4 km) and overnight there before continuing to Santiago.

Or continue directly to Santiago along **Stage 5** to Sigüeiro (p.72).

Reflections:

Hidra de Xerusalém, Cambre

Iglesia de Santiago
A Coruna

CAMINO INGLÉS from **A CORUÑA** / *LA CORUÑA* / CORUNNA

A Coruña is the provincial capital and a thriving metropolis since medieval times when it served as the capital of the kingdom of Galicia. It has a vibrant population of 250,000 (the largest in Galicia). The pilgrim route from A Coruña is currently undertaken by a small band of pilgrims but interest is growing and numbers are set to increase now that the route allows pilgrims to apply for a compostela; *providing the applicant has evidence that they have walked the additional distance in their country of origin to reach the minimum 100 km required by the Pilgrim Office.* The route from A Coruña is only 74.9 km so the applicant requires proof they have walked at least an additional 25 km (an extra day of average walking). A letter from your local church or confraternity will suffice. If you are coming from the UK you can contact the Confraternity of St. James: *www.csj.org.uk* or the British Pilgrimage Trust: *www.britishpilgrimage.org* for details of available pilgrim routes and stamps. Irish pilgrims can contact the Camino Society Ireland: *www.caminosociety.com* A novel alternative is to include this stage from A Coruña as part of the pilgrimage from Ferrol.

If you don't choose to walk from A Coruña it is still well worth making a visit to the city with its historic links to the camino. **Arrival: bus** service from Santiago (Monbus / Alsa) and stops in Mesón do Vento (opp. Hotel Canaima). Journey time +1 hour / cost ±€10. Taxi 50 mins ±€120 (halve time and cost from Mesón). Fast train service takes only 30 minutes costs €10+.

The modern harbour area is well maintained while the old city boasts some wonderful sites including the medieval **Church of Santiago** (see photo opposite) so evocative of this ancient way. The nearby **Xardín San Carlos** houses the tomb of Sir John Moor who died defending A Coruña against the French in 1809 *(see photo below)*. The central square is known as **Plaza María Pita** named after a notable heroine in the defense of Coruña, this time against the English, in 1589. A British soldier was making his way to the highest part of the wall to plant the English flag when Maria Pita beat him to it declaring: *Quen teña honra, que me siga "Whoever has honour, follow me!"* Whereupon the English incursion was driven back by the defenders and the siege abandoned. Further around the peninsular is the only extant Roman lighthouse in the world **Torre de Hercules** *(photo next page)* a World Heritage Site with modern art installations. The city of A Coruña *Roman Brigantium* was an important strategic enclave on the maritime route between the mediteranean and northern Europe. Julius Caesar came here in 62 BCE to oversee the trade routes. While A Coruña was not an administrative capital, it was an important commercial and naval centre. The Roman Via XX joined A Coruña to Caldas de Reis on the Portuguese way and Lucus Augusti (Lugo) on the Camino Primitivo.

Puerto de A Coruña

❶ A CORUÑA *Turismo:* Plaza de María Pita © 981 923 093. Open :10:00-14:00 & 16:00-20:00. **❶** *Turismo Kiosco* Jardín de Méndez Núñez.

Monumentos Históricos: ❶ *Castelo S. Anton* & artillery museum. **❷** *Xardín San Carlos & tomb of Sir John Moore* opp. *Museo Histórico Militar.* **❸** *Igrexa de Santiago XII* credencial available (11:30–13:00 18:30 –19:30) + *adj. Cofradía Casa Rectoral with pilgrim information Thurs 19:00–21:00.* **❹** *Plaza de Maria Pita with turismo and* **Concello** *(see photo>).* **❺** *Torre de Hercules II adj.* **Menhires Polo Paz** *photos below.*

Lodging *central*: *(Note: there is currently no dedicated pilgrim albergue but numerous hotels/hostels are available. Some central options are listed below, an online search will show numerous additional options).*
❶ *Hs* **Alboran** *x30* €35-50 © 881 304 170 c/Riego de Agua 14. **❷** *Hs* **Hotil** €25 © 981 976 302 r/Galera. **❸** *Hs* **Mara** €30+ 981 221 802 r/Galera. On *Rúa Nueva* @*Nº*16 **❹** *Hs¨* **Carbonara** *x14* €35+ © 981 225 251 *www.hostalcarbonara.com* . @*Nº*7 **❺** *H¨* **La Provinciana** *x20* €38-48 © 981 220 400 *www.laprovinciana.net* @*Nº*3 **❻** *P¨* **Roma** *x20* €38-48 © 981 228 075 *www.pensionroma.com.* **❼** *H¨* **S.Catalina** *x30* €34+ © 981 226 704 *www.hotelstacatalina.es* c/Catalina. **❽** *H¨* **Nido** *x48* €35-45 © 981 213 201 r/San Andrés 146. **❾** *H¨¨¨* **Zenit** *x70* €68+ © 912 182 028 r/Cmte Fontanes 18. **❿** *H¨¨¨¨* **Riazor** *x174* €79+ © 981 253 400 A./Pedro Barrie de la Maza, 29.

Menhires Pola Paz

Torre de Hercules

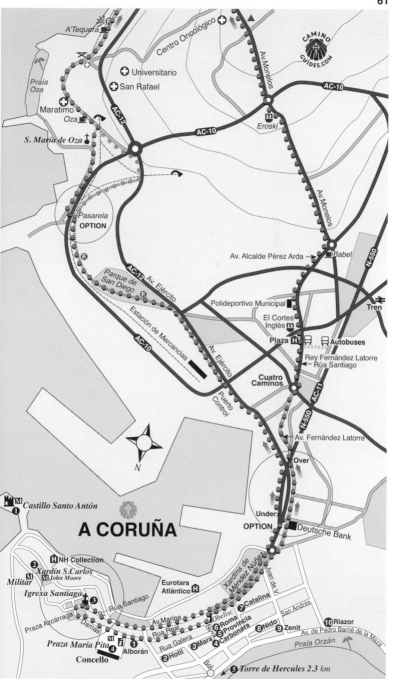

1a A CORUÑA – HOSPITAL de BRUMA

Santiago 74.9 km *(46.5 ml)*

┉┉┉┉	--- ---	10.1	--- --- ---	48%
────	--- ---	16.7	--- --- ---	51%
▬▬▬▬	--- ---	<u>6.1</u>	--- --- ---	1%
Total km	--- ---	**32.9** km *(20.4 ml)*		

Total ascent **980**m ±1½ *hr*

Alto.*m* ▲ A Malata **460**m *(1509 ft)*

< Ⓐ Ⓗ > ➲ Cambre: **13.8.9** km ➲ Sergude: **19.9** km

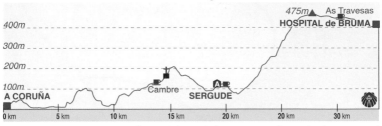

The Practical Path: The first 14 km of this stage is through the city and suburbs along busy main roads and dangerous sections of the N-550. Waymarking is limited and has to compete with other street signs so extra vigilance is needed. An attractive alternative along the coast is available and full details are included in this guide. Whichever route you take this makes for a very long and demanding stage if attempted in one day so almost all pilgrims opt to stay either in the new municipal albergue in **Sergude** or in **Cambre** on the alternative route which also offers the opportunity to visit the Templar 'chalice' in Cambre linked to the biblical miracle at Cana. Facilities on the last 20 km are limited so take energy snacks and plenty of water.

The Mystical Path: *The only impossible journey is the one you never begin. Anthony Robbins.* It is easy to let expectations and reservations run riot in our minds before commencing a journey of Self discovery. Yet the only effective way to answer any doubts is to simply start, experience and finally see. Stepping out helps to calm the mind and brings us present to the miracle of present moment awareness – the quiet certainty of the here and now. All we need is an open heart and open mind...all else follows naturally and everything becomes apparent as we proceed in faith.

0.0 km **Igrexa de Santiago** the 'new' official waymarked route no longer proceeds down rua Santiago to the harbour but turns back into Praza do Xeneral Azcárraga and down Rua Damas and Calle Ángeles into **Praza de María Pita [0.3** km] magnificent square with Casa do Concello ❶*Turismo sello* & public toilets in centre. Continue straight (not diagonally) through the square into pedestrianised Rúas Riego de Agua (parallel to harbour road

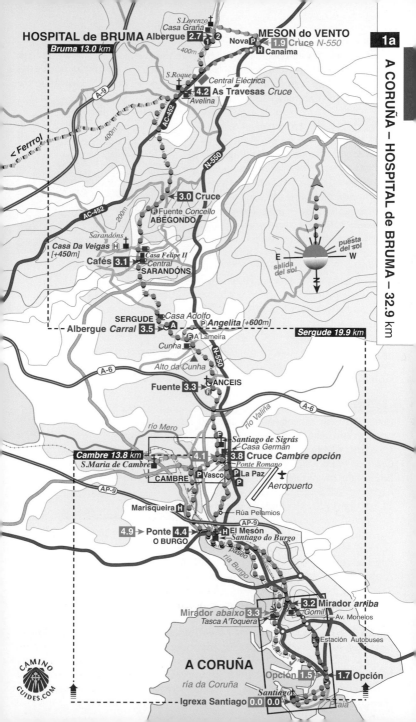

S.Lorenzo
Casa Graña **2.7** 2
HOSPITAL de BRUMA Albergue 1
Bruma 13.0 km Nova P **1.9** Cruce *N-550*
MESON do VENTO
H Canaima
400m

S.Roque *Central Eléctrica*
4.2 **As Travesas** *Cruce*
Avelina

AC-452
400m
< Ferrrol
A-9

N-550

3.0 Cruce
Fuente *Concello*
ABEGONDO
AC-452
200m

Sarandóns
Casa Da Veigas H
[+450m]
Cafés **3.1**
Casa Felipe II
Central
SARANDÓNS

E
puesta del sol
W
salida del sol

SERGUDE *Casa Adolfo*
A
Albergue *Carral* **3.5** P *Angelita* [+600m]
Sergude 19.9 km
Cunha A Lameira

A-6
Alto da Cunha
N-550

Fuente **3.3** CANCEIS

río Valiña
A-6
río Mero

Santiago de Sigrás
Casa Germán
Cambre 13.8 km **4.1** **3.8** Cruce *Cambre opción*
S.Maria de Cambre *Ponte Romano*
CAMBRE P Vasco P La Paz P
Aeropuerto

AP-9
Marisqueira H
Rúa Pelamios

4.9 Ponte **4.4** H El Mesón
O BURGO *Santiago do Burgo*

paseo
ría Burgo

3.2 Mirador *arriba*
Gomil
Mirador *abaixo* **3.3**
Tasca A'Toquera
Av. Monelos

Estación Autobuses

A CORUÑA
ría da Coruña
Opción **1.5** **1.7** Opción
Santiago
Igrexa Santiago **0.0** **0.0**
Praia

CAMINO
GUIDES.COM

on alt. route) past •*P Alboran* Rua Real onto the Avenida Marina by **obelisk** [**0.6** km]. Keep s/o (straight on) towards Gadis sign to **Deutsche Bank** [**0.8** km]. *Option here to join alt. coastal route green arrow below* ▬➡ Continue s/o by pedestrian crossing just *before* the N-550 flyover.

1.7 km N-550 flyover *opción* (*See green panel page 66 for alt. route* ▬➡). For waymarked route keep s/o *up* and take the next pedestrian crossing *over* the **N-550** [**0.2** km] *(yellow arrow in photo>)* and into Av. Fernández Latorre and down into ***Parque y Rotunda Cuatro Caminos*** [**0.4** km] with central fountain. Keep s/o past rear of central **bus station** *estación de*

autobuses [**0.4** km] past Cortes El Inglés and Escuelas Deportivas Municipias (left) to next **roundabout** [**0.5** km] with steel interlaced 'tribute' to the confluence of the city with Monelos river *Simboliza el homenaje de la ciudad al rio Monelos*. Essentially this marks the start of a long hard slog up Avenida Monelos onto a series of major road intersections relieved, somewhat, by views over the estuary at the top. Continue up past Eroski supermarket s/o uphill past Repsol Garage (right). This marks the high point and we now head downhill on Av. de Montserrat past •*Hs* **Lopez** *x4* €30 ✆ 652 059 518 to café Gomil and **viewpoint** [**1.7** km] over the expansive estuary.

3.2 km **Mirador** *arriba* 🍴 *Gomil* (left) with fine views down over the estuary and ornate spire of *Igrexa La Baca* visible directly below adj. *Centro Oncológico*. Keep s/o into Av. de Pedralonga and continue along the *left* verge (*see photo*) of **overpass AC-11** [**0.9** km] *[!]* . Continue along the

N-555 and veer left and s/o into r/A.E. Carballo in *O Portádego* [*+400m* •*H*````**Crunia** *x33* €66-80 ✆ 981 650 088 and •*H*``**A Barquiña** *x28* €35-45 ✆ 981 662 402 *www.abarquina.es*] continue down to **roundabout** [**1.5** km] and left to 2nd roundabout to continue down Av. Xoán Carlos I to ***Paseo da Ría do Burgo*** [**0.6** km].

*[Detour 100m right over pasarela to Tide Mill **Acea da Má** that used the force of the tides to power the mill, one of the oldest in Galicia, dating back to King Fernando II in the 12th century, reconstructed in the 16th and abandoned at the end of 20th. Now restored as the Museo dos Muíños on rio Trabe].*

Join the alternative coastal route by the estuary in the **Botanical gardens** and **Paseo da Ría do Burgo**. Continue along the estuary path to **O Burgo bridge** [**1.4** km] in ***Culleredo***.

4.4 km **Puente O Burgo** *opción*
[The bridge has Roman origins, part of the Via XX through Caldas de Reis and Lucus Augusti (Lugo) but was rebuilt in the medieval period with further works after its partial destruction by English troops under Sir John Moore in their attempt to halt the French here in 1809]. (▼Alt. river route branches off left here see green panel on p.66)

▲Those taking the official waymarked route now have another long slog along the N-550 and parallel roads around A Coruña airport. At roundabout turn up right past ⑪ *Mesón A Cepa* opp. ***Igrexa de Santiago del Burgo*** *XII* [**0.1** km]. *[This emblematic Church once administered to pilgrims arriving by boat as far back as the 12th century. It belonged to the order of the Temple, along*

Igrexa Santiago *O Burgo*

with the church of Santa Maria do Temple on the far side of river, but is now incongruously surrounded by traffic & hoardings]. Cross over rail to roundabout **O Burgo** *Culleredo* with •*Hs¨* **El Mesón** *x14* €30+ ✆ 981 660 065 adj. •*P¨***Casa Julio** *x9* €40+ ✆ 981 660 089. Turn left under AP-9 motorway and up right> into **Rúa Pelamios** [**0.7** km] into Rúa San Xiao past *Igrexa San Xiao De Almeiras* rest area & **cruceiro** [**0.6** km] keep s/o uphill (airport visible right) into Rúa Choeira past sports hall and turn left into Rúa Arcebispo Xelmirez. We now begin our descent with views over the industrial estates below down to join road parallel to the **N-550** [**1.5** km] [⑪/*P¨* **A Gramalleira** *x6* ✆981665076 and •*P¨***La Paz** *x15* €20-€30 ✆ 981 650 101 opp. side of N-550]. Turn left at roundabout and imm. turn right onto track down to cross over **Ponte Romano** [**0.6** km] over río Valiñas and up to **A Xira crossroads** [**0.3** km].

3.8 km **Cruce** *Cambre Opción*▲▼
⑪ *Casa Germán (right +50m) [Alternative river route left +400m via* •*P* **Mesón Vasco** *+*⑪ *see next page for details and **detour to Cambre**].*
▲Keep s/o at crossroads *[!]* up past shrine to St. Anthony *Si Buscas milagros, Mira!* "If you seek miracles, look!" to **Igrexa de Santiago** Sigrás [**0.6** km] (photo>). [☞] The XVth century

pilgrim hostel may not serve pilgrims today but does preserve the historical link to the medieval pilgrims who rested here. The buildings retain a variety of styles with Romanesque predominant.

●●●● **Coast and river option to Sigrás:** *Attractive alternative (not currently signposted. However, it follows the estuary all the way around the coast to O Burgo and thence by riverside path to Cambre)* **13.8** km *-versus-* **13.1** km on the official route along busy main roads around the airport. *Note:* The first 4.8 km are most clearly shown on the A Coruña town plan on page 61.

0.0 km Igrexa de Santiago From the beautiful main (West) door of the church with image of Santiago Matamoros in the tympanum (photo>)proceed down rua Santiago into Av. Marina and harbour front. From this point we follow the coast always on our left until we reach O Burgo (*note* at times we are excluded from the actual seafront by the security fence around the commercial harbour). Continue along Av. Marina through gardens *Xardíns de Méndez Núñez* to main port gate (left) and pedestrian crossing (right) imm. *before* N-550 flyover and option.

1.5 km N-550 flyover *paso elevado* **opción** With main gate to the port (left) take the *first* section *only* of the pedestrian crossing (right) to sweep around to our left *under* the N-550 (green arrow on photo page 64). *[Note main waymarked route continues s/o at this point by Deutsche Bank building to cross the N-550 higher up – yellow arrow].*
For alt. route follow the pavement around to the left *under* flyover with the main road (AC-12) on our right and the harbour railing on our left. Keep s/o past entrance to Port railhead *Puerto Control* (left) along cycle/pedestrian track and turn left *into* **Parque de San Diego** [**1.2** km] *Cemento Cosmos (left)*. Continue along Paseo Marineiro on cycle/pedestrian track (railway below) through the park with several drinking fonts [⛲] and statues to pedestrian bridge (left) **pasarela** [**0.8** km] and **option:** *[●To continue by road (400m longer) keep s/o along track to main road & turn left along pavement down under access road & over rail to join the beach road by cafe Oza].*

For beach option take the pasarela over rail down to Puerto de Ozo and turn right alongside railway towards city beach *Playa de Oza* [*Note: if you intend to walk the beach or swim here be aware that a high cliff at the end of the beach prevents further continuation this way].* Take the gate to the right of *Igrexa de Santa María de Oza* up steps to the road by railway and university faculty of *Fisioterapia* [**0.9** km] & ⛲ *Oza* with rear terrace. Keep s/o past *Hospital Marítimo de Oza* until road veers left and narrows into lane Xubias de *Abaixo* (chemist *right* picnic area *left*) down to **viewpoint** [**0.4** km].

3.3 km Mirador *Abaixo* ☕*Tasca A'Toquera* with fine views over the estuary and [☕]. Continue uphill to join the AC-12 at **Hospital Teresa Herrera** [**0.5** km]. Turn left and follow cycle/pedestrian track by main road past ⁋*Terraza* to **bridge** [**1.1** km]. Take steps *this* side of bridge down and turn right along the estuary promenade past old defaced waymark *mojón* by **pasarela** [**1.3** km] [***Detour*** +300m to •*Hotel* **Crunia** €50 ℂ *981 650 088 Av. Fonteculler, 58*]. Keep s/o along estuary wall (inlet on right) to where the rio Trabe flows out under the rail line from the *Tide Mill of Acea da Má (see page 64 for details)* and the official waymarked route joins [**0.7** km]. Both routes now merge and continue along the *Paseo Ria Do Burgo* estuary wall before separating again at O Burgo bridge [**1.3** km].

4.9 km Puente O Burgo *opción [For main route turn right – see previous page].* To continue via the river route take the historic stone bridge over the río Mero estuary and turn right along the river bank by ☕*Casa Leonardo* on Paseo Templarios. (*Igrexa Santa Maria do Temple* 100m). Continue along the *Sendeiro do Mero / Roteiro Mariñán* by the river under AP-9 motorway to •*H⁺A´***Marisqueira** €35 ℂ 981 664 101 Rúa Barcala [**1.3** km]. Opp. hotel take the delightful riverside path which we follow (past *embalse Telva*) until it meets the main road by **bridge** [**2.1** km] (**Puente 0.0** on map below) Turn right (green arrows below) to follow road to roundabout [**0.3** km] and •*P⁺⁺***Mesón Vasco** €18-32+ (pilgrim discount) ℂ981 661 202 +⁋ Lugar de la Telva. A good place to stay if you plan to visit Cambre (details next page). Continue s/o (chemist left) to join main route at crossroads [**0.4** km]:

4.1 km Cruce *Cambre Opción* Turn up left for Sigrás (yellow arrows).

CAMBRE · *Igrexa S.María de Cambre* · Castro · Concello · Taxi · Policia · río Mero · *Igrexa Santiago Sigrás* · *Antiguo hospital de peregrinos* · Cruce → Casa Germán · Ponte Romano · P ⁋ Meson Vasco · río Valiñas · Puente 0.0 km → · ◀ *Igrexa S.María 1.4 km* · *Igrexa Santiago Sigrás 1.3 km*

Detour CAMBRE 1.4 *km (±20 mins.)* ● ● ● ● A wonderful opportunity to visit the *Roman Villae* & Cambre church with its links to the Order of the Temple and the stone receptacle allegedly used by Jesus in his first miracle *the turning of water into wine at the marriage of Canna in Galilee*. Brought here from Jesusalem by a Templar Knight. This being the only relic in *Galicia* directly associated with the life of Christ. Perhaps, in time, it will become known as the *camino do Cristo*. The delightful town of Cambre is a pleasant 20 minute walk through ancient oak forests. This detour can be gracefully incorporated by walking from A Coruña to Cambre (±14 km), overnighting at **Mason Vasco** (details previous page) and continuing to Bruma the following day (± 20.4 km).

Directions From the bridge over the **río Mero** [**0.0**m] turn left and just *before* the rail bridge take the earth **path** [**200**m] right through oak woods ⮕ (see photo>) parallel to the railway and turn up left on **road** [**400**m] and imm. left again *over* railway into rua Canteira and at far end keep s/o to **path** [**200**m] (PRG-17 yellow and white blaise) through oak woods and turn up right onto concrete access lane to **Policia Local** [**500**m] and head up steps to the right to **church** [**100**m] **TOTAL 1.4** km.

Igrexa Santa María de Cambre *XII. Beautifully preserved XIIth romanesque church with the stone chalice **Hidra de Xerusalém**. The lip of the receptacle has been worn smooth by the hands of countless pilgrims over the centuries. The apse has an ambulatory typical of pilgrim churches and influenced by the cathedral of Santiago. The tympanum in the western façade is framed by two buttresses with the symbol of The Lamb of God Agnus Dei. The keystone of the archivolt is a figure of Daniel. The entire is balanced with a lovely rose window. The interior has finely carved figurines and animal motifs adorning the capitals. The church is open daily 10:00 – 21:00 (19:00 in winter). Opp. the West door is the archaeological Museum and Tourist office on Praza do Mosteiro* ℭ *981 656 217. Apart from its links to the English pilgrim way Cambre was also a Roman settlement with notable baths. There are several pleasant cafes and a taxi rank adjacent. Return the same way.*

▲ From the crossroads *Cruce Cambre Opción [¶ Casa Germán right +50m and ¶ Meson Vasco left +400m]* Keep s/o past roadside shrine *Buscas Milagros Mira* to **Igrexa de Santiago de Sigrás [0.6 km]** [⚑] and adj. medieval pilgrim hostal (photo p.65). Continue s/o along quiet roads past lavandeira & [⚑] (right) and cross the **A-6 motorway [1.6 km]** and turn left along country lane into the ancient hamlet of **Anceis [1.1 km]**.

3.3 km Fuente *Anceis* [⚑] drinking font by Pazo (see photo>). Continue through plaza San Marcos with stone cruceiro. We now head onto a lovely stretch of path into the municipality of Carral famous for its 'Martyrs of Liberty'... and its bread! The latter from the abundance of wheat found in this locality and ground in stone mills *albeiros*. We have a sampling opportunity in the **hilltop café [1.7 km]** ☕ *Panaderia Da Cunha*. Keep s/o downhill past covered **rest area [0.4 km]** [⚑] **A Lameira** to **crossroads [0.2 km]** *[Detour s/o 600m (sign Sayáns Cebral) to N-550 in Tabeaio •P⁺Angelita x9 €30-45 © 981 671 147 & •P⁺Mesía x5 €18-28 © 981 670 460]* Turn left for waymarked route into **Sergude [1.2 km]**

3.5 km Sergude *Carral* ●*Alb.* **Sergude-***Carral* *Xunta.* *[30÷2]* €10. Modern Xunta hostal with all facilities. Keep s/o downhill past ☕ *Casa Adolfo* (right). We enter the Parroquia San Xulián de Segude *[who proudly proclaim that Cosimo Medici passed through here on his way*

to England (1669) followed by English author of 'The Bible in Spain' George Borrows (1803 – 1881)]. We next enter delightful mature oak and chestnut woods around Parroquia Santa Baia de Cañás *[who, not to be outdone in the celebrity stakes, proclaims that the spring water from here was known for its miraculous healing properties]*... and into Sarandóns.

3.1 km Sarandóns ☕ *Centro* opp. Capilla de San Juan 1657. Keep s/o along main street passing *Casa Felipe*. *[Nᵒ14 housed Felipe II on his way to A Coruña from where he sailed to England to marry Queen Mary in 1554]*. Pass ☕ *Bar A Taberna* to crossroads **[0.4 km]**. *[Detour left +450m off route past church of Sarandóns to •H⁺Casa Das Veigas x8 €80+ ©981 671 616 www. casadasveigas.es]*. Keep s/o (right) via quiet country lanes past *Concello de Abegonda* [⚑] **[1.8 km]** to cross of 5 roads **crossroads [0.8 km]**.

3.0 km Cruce *A Cruz de Beira [Several pazos in the area sheltered royalty in their travels and also the notorious tribute of the one hundred maidens* El tribute de las cien doncellas *who were allegedly held in nearby tower of Bordel pending exile as a 'gift' by King Mauregato to prevent the Muslim Caliphate in Córdoba from invading. Carrión de los Condes on the camino Francés has a similar legend].* Turn *up* left to merge onto forest track through eucalyptus **woods [0.6** km] which continue for 2.2 kilometres to cross main road from Betanzos [**!**] **AC-542 [2.2** km] onto track and continue back to re-join AC-542 [**1.0** km] where the route from Ferrol joins from the left. Continue along main road into **As Travesas [0.4** km].

4.2 km Cruce *As Travesas* 🍴 *Casa Avelina* popular pilgrim halt with welcome from Maria Carmen Ⓒ 981 630 262. *[Pick-up for guests staying at Hotel Canaima].* Opposite is a small chapel dedicated to *San Roque – site of local pilgrimage in August].* We now have a long (1.6 km) slog on the busy AC-542 *[!]* past the *Red Eléctrica de España* at the end of which is a detour (100m) down side road (right) to a Celtic Castro **Eira dos Mouros,** one of the largest castros in Galicia dating back to the 4th century BCE. *[Mouros generally refers to mythical beings who lived underground, often associated with archaeological mounds and the faery folk and **not** with the Moors of North Africa].* Nothing much remains of the site which was excavated to reveal some Roman artefacts. We pass this side road continuing s/o past Repsol depot (left) and turn <left by abandoned **Galp station [1.6** km] onto track through woodland to join quiet country lane into **Bruma [1.2** km]: *[Note: If you are staying in **Meson do Vento** it is possible to continue s/o along the main road by the Galp turn-off but it is recommended to take the safer but longer waymarked route via Bruma].*

2.8 km **Hospital de Bruma** peaceful hamlet with ultra modern albergue ❶*Alb.* **San Lorenzo** *Priv. [22÷4]* €20 +2 €55 Ⓒ 619 464 240 *www. alberguesanlorenzobruma.com* all facilities. In stark contrast to the pilgrim hostel opp. ❷*Alb.* **Bruma** *Xunta. [22÷3]* €10 Ⓒ 981 692 921 sensitively restored and occupying a tranquil riverside site. Popular 🍴/🍴 *Casa Graña* (100m) Ⓒ981 696 006 with menú peregrino adj. medieval chapel of *San Lorenzo (part dating to XIIc).* [●●●*Alt. lodging 1.9 km off route in **Meson do Vento** details p.56]. Directions from **Bruma – Sigüeiro – Santiago** next page.

Albergue de Bruma

Reflections:

_____
_____
_____
_____
_____
_____
_____
_____
_____
_____
_____
_____
_____
_____
_____
_____
_____
_____
_____
_____
_____
_____
_____
_____
_____
_____
_____
_____
_____
_____
_____
_____
_____
_____

5 HOSPITAL de BRUMA – SIGÜEIRO

Santiago 42.0 km *(26.1 ml)*

┄┄┄┄┄	--- ---	10.3	--- ---	41%
▬▬▬▬	--- ---	13.6	--- ---	54%
▬▬▬▬	--- ---	1.3	--- ---	5%
Total km	--- ---	**25.6** km	*(15.9 ml)*	

Total ascent **340**m ±½ *hr*

Alto.m ▲ Cabeza de Lobo **430**m *(1410 ft)*

< 🅰 🄷 > ➲A Rua **7.1** km ➲Poulo **9.5** km.

The Practical Path: A gentle stage as we descend towards **Sigüeiro**. The majority is spent on quiet country lanes and woodland paths offering shade. New waymarking from Baixoia now runs alongside the AP-9 which can be avoided by taking the 'old' (green) route through delightful woodland to emerge at the industrial outskirts of Sigüeiro where both routes join. Our destination is a thriving modern town with strong industrial base making a stark contrast to the rural landscape we have been immersed in until now. The modernity of Sigüeiro is softened by the Río Tambre and its tributary that flows through the town's peaceful parkland. For those looking to break up this stage the albergue in Poulo now provides a good midway stopover.

The Mystical Path: *Even in the midst of life's many storms we have the capacity to stand in the centre of our own peace.* As we near the end of our journey we need to prepare to reintegrate back into life, *in the fast lane.* How can we retain the calm and clarity found along the way with the challenges & busyness of our everyday lives?
I rose with the sun and left in the quiet of the new day. The dawn chorus was the only sound that accompanied me through the shaded woodland paths. As I approached Sigüeiro the soft path underfoot changed from earth to unyielding asphalt and the harsh reality and bustle of... an industrial estate.

0.0 km **Hospital de Bruma** from albergue ❷ pass 🍴*Casa Graña* and *capela San Lorenzo* (left) and keep s/o through **O Seixo** *[where pilgrims staying in Meson do Vento join from the right]* and s/o through **Cabeza de Lobo** roadside cross *cruceiro* and *Igrexa San Pedro de Ardemil* (left) into **Cruz**:

3.6 km **Cruz** *Cruce* hamlet straddling crossroads with 🍴*Uzal* and giant statue of Santiago. Keep s/o past roadside sculpture park and follow quiet

5 HOSPITAL de BRUMA – SIGÜEIRO – 25.6 km

CAMINO GUIDES.COM
Miras
A
2.0 Centro
SIGÜEIRO
Rio Tambre
DP-3801
Industrial
Televés
Alt. 4.7 Cruce 5.5
AC-461
Seoane +1.4 km
Cepsa
Rio Lenguelle
Fonte da Santiña
F
6.1 Túnel opción
BAIXOIA
N-550
S
W puesta del sol
salida del sol E
N
Rego da Ponte Ribeira
Ponte Ribeira
AP-9
ORDES
Cruceiro
2.5 Café
Casa Felipe II
CALLE (POULO)
< 2.5 km >
Alda Camiño Inglés
Outeiro de Abaixo POULO
Casa Rectoral
Louro [+2.5 km]
Albergue 2.4
A
C
Anton Veiras
Linares A Rua
Iglesia San Palayo
A Rua 3.5
C Dona Maria
Nova
A RUA
F
< 1.8 km >
Barreiro +2.0 km
Castrelos
Uzul
F
CRUZ
3.6 Cruce
AP-9
San Pedro de Ardemil
CABEZA DE LOBO
N-550
O SEIXO
MESON doVENTO
San Lorenzo
Café Casa Graña
Novo
P
Canaima
HOSPITAL de BRUMA
2
0.0 Albergue

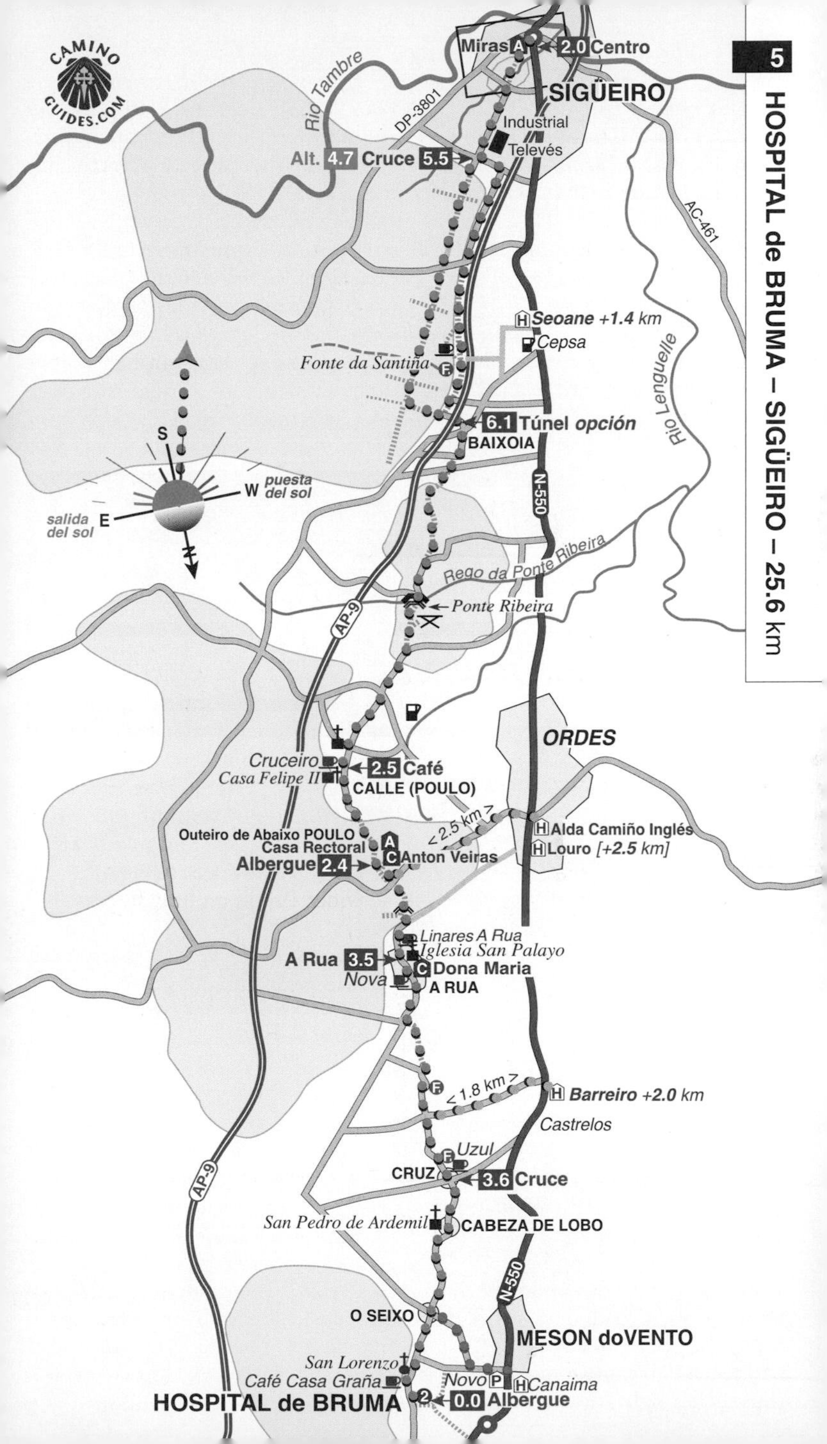

road to next crossroads.*[Detour Castrelos N-550 right +1.8 km (3.6 km return!) •Hotel Barreiro x45 €35-55 © 981 680 917 www.hotelbarreiro.com* Continue past [🚰] *Fonte da Carballeira* then onto short stretch of earth path to rejoin country road into the village of **A Rua**.

3.5 km   A Rua welcoming 🍴 *Bar Novo* opp. •CR **Dona Maria** *x5* €55+ © 981 681 430 *www.casadonamaria.es* A Rúa. Keep s/o through the village past *Igrexa San Pelayo* (right) *[with 18th century statue on gable wall of the child martyr Pelayo, martyred during the caliphate of Abderraman III]*. Just beyond the church is 🍴*Bar Linares*. Keep s/o before veering right through houses then back to main road to turn <left onto quiet path. Cross bridge over *Rego do Cabo* and continue through woodland. Cross main road and shortly after is right turn *(off route 40m)* to luxury •*CR* **Antón Veiras** *x6* €60+© 981 682 303 *www.casaruralantonveiras.*

es adj. to the refurbished *casa rectoral* albergue (photo>) ●*Alb.* **Casa Rectoral de Poulo** *Xunta [42÷1]* €10 © 676 966 461. *[Detour Ordes +2.5km on N-550 right. •H¨***Alda Camiño Inglés** *x28* €30+ ©*881 073 934 / •Hs¨***Louro** *x7* €15+ ©*981 680 831]*. The waymarked route re-joins a country road before entering **A Calle**.

4.9 km   A **Calle** ancient roadside cross by 🍴 *O Cruceiro* welcome stop run by by Carolina from England and her Galician husband. This is the *'last chance saloon'* for something to eat or drink before Sigüeiro. *[Note: left of the cafe is a non-descript building worth a look. 'Behind' the open porch is a lintel with the coat of arms of* **Felipe II** *who*

spent a night here. The only sign for this historical link to the past is a dedication to the local Mayor! Philip II (1556–98) was arguably the most influential king of Spain and Portugal and champion of the Roman Catholic Counter-Reformation. He was also de facto king of England and Ireland through his marriage to Queen Mary! **Cosimo de Medici III** *also passed here in 1669 on his way to A Coruña to England having just completed his pilgrimage to Santiago. Cosimo III was the longest ruling Medici and a great patron of the Arts. It is for good reason the road we are on is called the Royal Road 'Calle Real'.]*

Continue past parish church *Virgen de la Merced*. The route now alternates between quiet roads and woodland tracks to picnic area by medieval stone bridge *Rego da Ponte Ribeira* (easy to miss next to the modern road bridge beside it). Continue to crossroads at **Baixoia**. Continue s/o over crossroads (bus shelter right) down to underpass under the AP-9.

6.1 km   Túnel *Baixoia opción*. ▲▼New waymarks direct us (right) to track that runs alongside the busy AP-9 motorway. You can avoid this by taking the original shorter route through peaceful woodland tracks as follows:

● ● ● ● [**4.7** -v- **5.5** km] ▼50m after exiting the underpass keep s/o past new waymark (right) onto woodland track. At crossroads [**0.6** km] **turn right>** to continue straight on along wide straight track for **4.1** km until it rejoins the main route at bus shelter Concello de Oroso in *Lugar Oroso de Abaixo* [**4.7** km].

▲For the newly waymarked route turn sharp right (opp. farm building) back to AP-9 and turn down left this side of the motorway to continue parallel alternating between asphalt and track to covered drinking font [⛲] *Fonte da Santiña* [**1.6** km]. *[Its re-construction, to allow for the building of the motorway, belies its ancient history. Known for its divination and healing powers especially throat conditions – The throat chakra symbolises access to the spiritual realms, creative expression and divine will].* Father Martín Sarmiento mentions the fountain in his diaries of 1745.

Continue past sign for ▲*Glamping Corredoira do Camiño Inglés!* where *Xaquin (pron: Shakeen)* ✆ 609 951 615 is restoring an original stretch of the *camino primitivo* and plans to provides snacks and 'wild camping'. *[Detour Os Carballos N-550 right +1.4 km. •Hs Seoane x12 €35-45 ✆ 981 699 222].* Continue alongside AP-9 to emerge onto road [**3.5** km] (bridge over motorway right) and veer left down to join the alt. route at crossroads by bus shelter in *Lugar Oroso* [**0.4** km].

5.5 km   Cruce *Lugar Oroso de Abaixo* Turn right (s/o if have taken the alternative woodland route) by bus shelter through modern industrial estate with Televés building (right) and imm. past the Rua Camiño Inglés (left) turn left into town park and over footbridge Río Carboeiro. The waymarked route crosses the park past plaque to *Margery Kempe [14th century Christian visionary and mystic (born 1373). She was known for her deep devotional life and her diaries detailing her journey through life, became the first autobiography in English and the first record of a female pilgrim].* On the road parallel to the park is *Alb*❶ *Priv* **Segue o Camiño** *[20÷2]* €18 +1 €60 ✆ 613 379 963 www.segueocamino.com. To continue into town centre follow waymarks through the park to Praza Concello, then via the Rua Camiño Real past albergue Camiño Real to town centre:

`2.0 km` Sigüeiro *Centro* modern town with active industrial base and wide range of lodging, restaurants and cafés (see town plan).

Lodging Central: ❷*Alb. Priv.* **Camiño Real** *[18÷3]* €15 +2 €55 ⓒ 648 746 023 *www.caminorealsantiago. com* r/Ourense 9 & c/Real (photo>).

❸*Alb. Priv.* **Ultreia et Suseia** *(prev. Fogar da Chisca) [10÷1]* €15 +3 €45 ⓒ 638 177 894 r/Campo 4. ❹*Alb. Priv.* **Quinta Andaina** *[10÷1]* €15 ⓒ 609 075 482 Ave. da Grabanxa 28. ❺*Alb.* **Mirás** *[14÷4]* €15 (+¶) ⓒ 685 445 921 / 881 981 909 Av. Compostela (centro N-550). ❻*Hs* **Sigüeiro** *x9* €26-60 ⓒ 981 973 636 *www.sigueirohostel.com* Praza Alexandre Bóveda ultra-modern hostel with restaurant & rear terrace onto the Rio Tambre. ❼*Hs* **Siaba** *x7* €50+ ⓒ 666 530 791 *www.hostelsiaba.es* r/ da Insua, 1 •*Apt.***A Barciela** *x1* €70 (4 persons) ⓒ 680 977 914 Lg. Sigueiro 9-2B (far side of bridge on exit).

Lodging Outskirts: *+1.5 km North of town centre adj. the AP-9* •*P.* **Vilanova** *x6* €45+ ⓒ 630 125 544 *Alto de Vilanova N-550].*

Sigüeiro with an expanding population of 5,000 has become a modern 'dormitory' town of Santiago which is now only 16 km away. It has an expanding industrial base and increasing accommodation options, however, consider booking in advance during the busy summer season or be prepared to continue on to •*motel* **Punta Cana** (3.4 km) or •*Hotel* **San Vincente** (see next stage). The town straddles the river Tambre which we cross by the original stone bridge (modified) constructed in the 14th century on the orders of Fernán Pérez de Andrade though little remains of its medieval roots.

Reflections:

_____
_____
_____
_____
_____
_____
_____
_____
_____
_____
_____
_____
_____
_____
_____
_____
_____
_____
_____
_____
_____
_____
_____
_____
_____
_____
_____
_____
_____
_____
_____

Misty morning sunrise over Bruma:

6 SIGÜEIRO – SANTIAGO

16.4 km (10.2 ml) – Santiago

....	--- ---	8.3	--- ---	33%
————	--- ---	8.7	--- ---	50%
▬▬▬	--- ---	0.4	--- ---	17%
Total km	--- ---	**16.4** km		*(10.2 ml)*

▲ Total ascent **410**m ±¾ *hr*
Alto.m ▲ Garabal **390**m *(1280 ft)*
< Ⓐ Ⓗ > ➲ Formarís: **8.8** km

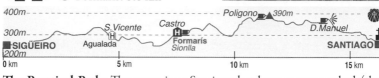

The Practical Path: The route into Santiago has been re-waymarked (the original way is shown in grey but is not recommended and waymarks will fade over time). The re-routing has reduced the overall distance to a relatively easy 16.4 km with 33% by forest paths, making for a pleasant entrance into the city. Hotel Castro does brisk pilgrim trade in its café around halfway (8.8 km). Extra vigilance is needed entering the city where waymarks compete for attention amongst other signage and fast moving traffic.

The Mystical Path: It is good to have an end to journey towards; but it is the journey that matters in the end. *Ernest Hemingway.*

While our camino might end in Santiago, our journey through life continues as we choose to have it be. Will the gentle pace of the camino stay with us or will we lose its sense of peace and purpose as we enter the bustle of Santiago and our life back at home. And where, on earth, is Home?

0.0 km Sigüeiro *Centro* Take N-550 out of town and cross Río Tambre *[Note: **Original route** ❷ took the first lane left (grey route on map) but waymarks at the start have been removed. It continues up past Iglesia San Andres by woodland paths to emerge at the back of hotel S. Vicente. Waymarks are now faded and it is easy to get lost in the maze of paths].* **New waymarks** ❶ now continue up the right hand side of the main road and turn right at the **Cepsa service station [0.6** km] to continue along quiet country lane parallel to the N-550 and **over AP-9 [0.9** km] which we cross to enter a short woodland track back to asphalt road and sign for **Vila Fernandez [2.1** km] *[**Detour left 250m** to •Motel **Punta Cana** €45 © 981 688 958 on N-550. Note the motel is opposite side of the busy and dangerous N-550. Take care if crossing].* Continue to discrete **crossroads [0.7** km].

4.3 km Cruce *La Meira [**Detour left 500m** sign for hotel •H***San Vicente

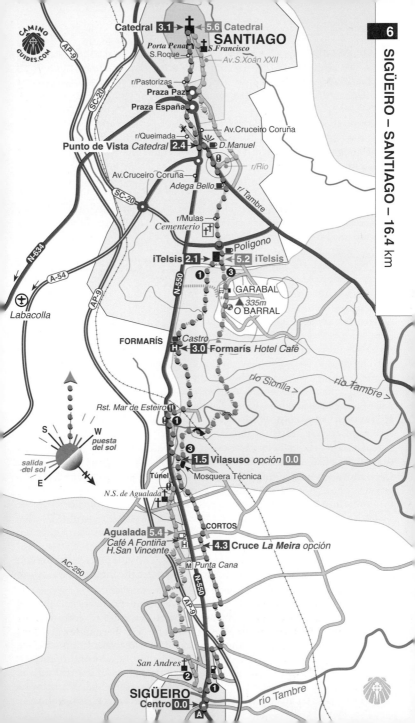

Catedral **3.1** ← **5.6** Catedral
SANTIAGO
Porta Pena ■ *S.Francisco*
S.Roque ○ ↑
Av.S.Xoán XXII

r/Pastorizas ○
Praza Paz
Praza España ●

r/Queimada ○ ✕
Punto de Vista *Catedral* **2.4** ●
Av.Cruceiro Coruña
● *D.Manuel*

Av.Cruceiro Coruña ○ 🅷
r/Río

Adega Bello ■
r/ Tambre

r/Mulas ○
Cementerio ☨
Polígono

iTelsis 2.1 ← ■ **5.2** iTelsis
❶ ❸
GARABAL
🅷 ▲*335m*
❷ **O BARRAL**

FORMARÍS *Castro*
🅷 ← **3.0 Formarís** *Hotel Café*

río Sionlla > *río Tambre >*

Rst. Mar de Esteiro ○
❶

❸
■ **1.5 Vilasuso** *opción* **0.0**
Túnel *Mosquera Técnica*
🅷
N.S. de Agualada ☨
CORTOS

Agualada 5.4 →
Café A Fontiña ○ 🅷 ← **4.3 Cruce** *La Meira* *opción*
H.San Vincente
Ⓜ *Punta Cana*

San Andres ☨
❷
❶
SIGÜEIRO
Centro 0.0
🅰 *río Tambre*

Labacola ✚

S W *puesta del sol*
salida del sol
E

CAMINO
GUIDES.COM

x18 €55-69 ⓒ 981 694 571 <u>*www.hotelsanvicente.com*</u> and adj. ☕ *A Fontiña* on N-550. *This is easily missed and only marked to provide an option for additional lodging if hostels in Sigüeiro were full. Again the hotel is the* **opposite** *side of the busy and dangerous N-550].*

Continue to next crossroads and turn up right in ***Cortos*** *No facilities*. The route now takes a left turn down a long straight stretch of country road to pass through a small residential neighbourhood in ***A Lameira*** to turn right onto a **woodland path** [**1.0** km]. *[**Original (grey) route** ❷ joins via N-550 underpass (visible left).* Continue on path to **T-Junction** [**0.5** km].

1.5 km **Vilasuso** *Option*. At nondescript T-junction (industrial building right *Mosquera Técnica de Aguas*) the newly waymarked route ❶ ▲ turns left over the small stream rego de Barcia.

The original route turned right at this point opp. Mosquera Técnica de Aguas and imm. <left onto tranquil paths to the outskirts of Santiago. This remote route is all by woodland tracks (see photo>). It is shown as ❸ on the map. Note their are NO facilities for 5.2 km. Again waymarks have been removed at the start and have become  faded elsewhere so this option is not recommended unless you have a good sense of direction and have additional time should you get lost.

Directions: from offices of Mosquera Técnica take the forest track opp. and turn right at next **junction** [**0.4** km] continue up left under **rail AVE** [**0.5** km] and follow the main forest track up to high point before it sweeps around to the right and down to the ***río Sionlla*** [**0.8** km]*(tributary of the río Tambre).* Cross the bridge and ascend the steep forest track (ignoring any tracks to right or left). As we crest the rise at 300m **turn left** [**1.6** km] (do **not** keep s/o at this point into As Pereiras). The track shortly turns into asphalt lane and we keep s/o through **staggered crossroads at O Barral** [**0.8** km] past [☕] (right) and s/o through next crossroads [**0.5** km] and shortly after we reach our high point 335m and **turn left by bus shelter** [**0.1** km] and original waymarker (opposite house with first floor glazed balcony) onto forest track to rejoin new waymarked route at **iTelsis** [**0.5** km] and enter the industrial estate and the busy ☕ *Poligono*. **Total 5.2 km.**

▲ To continue on the newly waymarked route turn left over the rego de Barcia to join lane that runs parallel to the busy N-550 which we use for a fraught 300m as we cross over the río Sionlla (the only other bridge crossing is on the alternative route). The road margin is narrow here and traffic fast moving [!]. We leave the N-550 at exclusive 🍽 *Mar de Esteiro* and up and over railway to enter a long stretch (3.5 km) of delightful woodland pathways *Bosque Encantado*. Halfway along is rear access to the hotel Castro and café.

3.0 km Formarís •*H***Castro** *x100*
€40-50 © 981 509 304 +☕ which
serves as a popular pilgrim stop! *www.
castrohotel.com*. Continue on forest
tracks alongside the río Salgueiro to
the edge of the industrial estate where
we turn up right to our high point
of today at ▲390m on the outskirts
of Santiago which we enter at the
iTelsis building, part of the modern
industrial estate *polígono industrial de
Tambre* and where the original route
now joins from our right:

2.1 km iTelsis ☕ *Polígono (sello)*. We now head over the main roundabout
to follow along the walls of Santiago cemetery (left) before descending Rua
Mulas to ☕ *Miro* & ☕ *Adega Bello* at junction of Rua Tambre which we
follow down past farmacia *(old signs show right turn here ●)* and •*P* **José Rey**
x9 €35-65 © 646 665 677 in **O Meixonfrío** +120 m. Continue s/o to ☕ *Bar
D. Manuel* with first view *punto da vista* of the towers of Santiago cathedral.

2.4 km **Punto de Vista**. Our route now veers sharp left to take a pedestrian
crossing over the dual carriageway *Av. Cruceiro Coruña N-550* into Rúa da
Queimada and imm. right [!] into Rúa dos Salgueiriños de Abaixo which we
follow down to pass the McDonalds ☕ at Praza de España. Cross over the
busy N-550 junction and head along the park area of Rúa de San Caetano to
the next major roundabout Praza da Paz.

Cross over and head down Rúa dos Basquiños then veer right into Rúa
Santa Clara (*hotel Santa Clara*) and into Rúa dos Loureiros (*hotels Altair*
and *Moure*) to Mirador Costa Vella *Porta da Pena* which marks the original
entrance to the city for pilgrims on the camino Inglés. Continue down into
Praza da Inmaculada under the palacio archway to Santiago cathedral.

3.1 km **Santiago** *Catedral Praza
do Obradoiro* Take time to 'arrive'. We
each experience different emotions at
coming to the journeys end. Gratitude
for safe arrival is a frequent response
but if we feel overwhelmed by the
crowds we can always return later – the
cathedral is generally open between
07:00 and 21:00. Whether now or
later and whichever door you entered
by, you might like to follow the time
worn pilgrim ritual described overleaf.
For Santiago city plan see page 89.

[1] Due to erosion it is no longer permitted to place your hand in the Tree of Jesse, the central column of the Master Mateo's masterpiece Door of Glory *Portico de Gloria*. But you can stop and admire the incomparable beauty of this inner portico carved between 1166 and 1188 (the exterior façade was added in 1750). The Bible and its main characters come alive in this remarkable storybook in stone. The central column has Christ in Glory flanked by the apostles and, directly underneath, St. James sits as intercessor between Christ and the pilgrim. Millions of pilgrims over the centuries have worn finger holes in the solid marble as a mark of gratitude for their safe arrival, the reason why it is now protected by a barrier. Proceed to the other side and where pilgrims of the past would touch their brow to that of Maestro Mateo, whose kneeling figure is carved into the back of the central column (facing the altar) and received some of his artistic genius in the ritual known as head-butting the saint *Santo d'Os Croques*. Proceed to the High Altar (right) to ascend the stairs and [2] hug the Apostle. Perhaps lay your head on his broad shoulders and say what you came here to say. Proceed down the steps on the far side to the crypt and the reliquary chapel under the altar. [3] Here, you can kneel before the casket containing the relics of the great Saint and offer your prayer ...

Pilgrim mass currently takes place four times per day; 07:30 / 09:30 / 12:00 / 19:30 (doors may close 5 minutes before on busy days). The swinging of the giant incense burner *Botafumeiro* was originally used to fumigate the sweaty (and possibly disease-ridden) pilgrims. The ritual requires half a dozen attendants *tiraboleiros* to perform it so has become a more infrequent event, details of special occasions when the *Botafumeiro* will be used can be found on the cathedral website (*www.catedraldesantiago.es*). You may also chance upon the spectacle if you happen to be in mass on a day when a private party has paid for the ritual to be performed, though these dates are not available in advance. The seating capacity has been extended to 1,000 so you might even find somewhere to sit but it is wise not to hold onto any expectations.

Reflections:

_____

_____

_____

_____

_____

_____

_____

_____

_____

_____

_____

_____

SANTIAGO *CITY* — 4 squares surround the cathedral, as follows:

● **Praza do Obradoiro**. The 'golden'
square of Santiago is usually thronged
with pilgrims and tourists admiring
the dramatic west facing façade of
the Cathedral, universal symbol of
Santiago, with St. James looking down
on all the activity from his niche in
the central tower. This provides the
main entrance to the Cathedral and
the Portico de Gloria. To the right of
the steps is the discrete entrance to the

museum. A combined ticket will provide access to all rooms including the
crypt and the cloisters and also to the 12th century palace of one of Santiago's
most famous individuals and first archbishop, Gelmírez *Pazo de Xelmírez*
situated on the (left). In this square we also find the beautiful Renaissance
façade of the Parador named after Ferdinand and Isabel *Hostal dos Reis
Católicos* on whose orders it was built in 1492 as a pilgrim hospice. Opposite
the Cathedral is the more austere neoclassical seat of the Galician government
and town hall *Pazo de Raxoi* with its solid arcade. Finally, making up the
fourth side of the square is the gable end of the *Colegio de S. Jerónimo* part
of the university. Moving anti-clockwise around the cathedral – turn up into
Rúa de Fonseca to:

● **Praza das Praterías**. The most
intimate of the squares with its lovely
centrepiece, an ornate statue of horses
leaping out of the water. On the corner
of Rúa do Vilar we find the Dean's
House *Casa do Deán* formerly the
pilgrim office. Along the walls of the
Cathedral itself are the silversmith's
plateros that give the square its name.
Up the steep flight of steps we come to
the magnificent southern door to the
Cathedral, the oldest extant doorway

and traditionally the entrance taken by pilgrims coming from Portugal. The
quality of the carvings and their arrangement is remarkable and amongst
the many sculptured figures is one of St. James between two cypress trees.
Continuing around to the right we come to:

● **Praza da Quintana**. This wide square is identified by the broad sweep of
steps separating the lower part *Quintana of the dead* from the upper *Quintana
of the living*. Opp the Cathedral is the wall of the *Mosteiro de San Paio de
Antealtares* (with museum of sacred art). The square provides the eastern
entrance to the Cathedral via the Holy Gate *Porta Santa* sometime referred

to as the Door of Pardon *El Perdón* only opened during Holy Years (this decade 2027 and 2032). Adjoining is the main entrance to the Cathedral shop with various guidebooks detailing the Cathedral's many chapels and their interesting carvings and statuary and the priceless artefacts and treasures in the museum. Finally, we head up the broad flight of steps around the corner and back into:

● **Praza da Inmaculada** to the north facing Azabachería façade, is the least well-known doorway and the only one that *descends* to enter the Cathedral. It has the most weathered aspect, with moss and lichen covering its bleak exterior. Opposite the cathedral is the imposing southern edifice of *Mosteiro de San Martiño Pinario* the square in front gets any available sun and attracts street artists. The archbishop's

arch *Arco Arzobispal* brings us back to the Praza do Obradoiro.

ⓘ The **Pilgrim Office** *Oficina del Peregrino*, Rua Carretas (*below the parador*) ⓒ 981 568 846 open daily 09:00-21:00 (10:00-20:00 winter). The office has a tight security procedure (expect lengthy delays) and may lack the informal atmosphere of the former office in Rua Vilar, but it is better suited to serve the ever growing pilgrim numbers and has all the facilities and advice a pilgrim could need. Providing you have fulfilled the criteria of a bona fide pilgrim and walked at least the last 100 km (200 km on bike or horseback) for religious/ spiritual reasons, collecting 2 stamps per day on your *credencial* you will be awarded the *Compostela* which may entitle you to certain privileges such as reduced entry fees to museums and a free meal at the Parador! If you do not fulfil the criteria you may still be able to obtain a **certificado** (€3) which is essentially a certificate of distance travelled. The welcoming Companions meet in a room upstairs and in the adjoining pilgrim chapel (see below).

●**The Camino Chaplaincy** offers Anglican services Sundays 12.30 at Igrexa de Santa Susana, parca da Alameda.
●**Camino Companions** based within the Pilgrims Office, offer reflective prayer in the pilgrims office *chapel* 11:30 and reflection and integration room 6, 1st floor 15:00 (both daily Mon-Sat). Mass in English daily (excl. Wednesdays) 10:30 also in the *chapel*.
●**Pilgrim House** rua Nova 19 also offers a place of welcome and reflection 11:00–20:00 (closed Wed & Sun) under the care of Terra Nova USA.

●**Pilgrim's Reception Office** Rúa das Carretas, 33. © 981 568 846 (*09:00-19.00*). ❶ *Turismo Centro*: r/ Vilar 63 © 981 555 129 *May-Oct: 09:00-19.00 (winter 17:00)* ● **Laundromat:** 09:00-22:00 **SC18** Rúa San Clemente 18 © 673 753 869. ● **Consignia Praca Quintana** (09:00-21:00) backpack storage €3 per day opp. Cath.● **Intermodal Central Train/Bus Station** 700m (10 mins) South of Praza Galicia.

Albergues: €10-€20 (*depending on season / beds per dormitory*) ❶–❾ (*on the camino Francés*). ❨**Rúa Concheiros** Nº48 ❿ **Santos** *Priv.[24÷3]* © 881 169 386. Nº36 ⓫ **La Estrella** *Priv.[24÷1]* © 881 973 926 *www.laestrelladesantiago. es* Nº10 ⓬ **Porta Real** *Priv.[20÷1]* © 633 610 114 *www.albergueportareal. es* ❨**Belvís +500***m* ⓭ **Seminario Menor** *Conv.[170÷30]*€16 *+81* €22-44 © 881 031 768 *www.alberguesdelcamino.com* Av. Quiroga Palacios . ❨**c/ S.Clara** ⓮ **LoopINN** (*La Salle*) © 981 585 667 c/ S.Clara. ⓯ **Meiga Backpackers** *Priv.[30÷5]* © 981 570 846 *www.meiga-backpackers.es* c/ Basquiños, 67.

Centro Histórico: ⓰ **Linares** *[14÷2]* © 981 943 253 r/ Algalia de Abaixo, 34. ⓱ **O Fogar de Teodomiro** *Priv.[20÷5]+* © 981 582 920 Plaza de Algalia de Arriba 3. ⓲ **The Last Stamp** *Priv.[62÷10]* © 981 563 525 r/ Preguntorio 10. ⓳ **Azabache** *Priv.[20÷5]* © 981 071 254 c/Azabachería 15. ⓴ **Km.0** *Priv.[50÷10]* © 881 974 992 *www.santiagokm0.es* r/ Carretas 11 (new renovation by pilgrim office) ㉑ **Blanco** *Priv.[20÷2]+4* €35-55 © 881 976 850 r/ Galeras 30. ㉒ **Mundoalbergue** *Priv.[34÷1]* © 981 588 625 c/ San Clemente 26. ❨*Otros:* ㉓ **La Estación** *Priv.[24÷2]* © 981 594 624 r/ Xoana Nogueira 14 (adj. rail station +**2.9** km). ㉔ **Compostela Inn** *Priv.[120÷30]+* © 981 819 030 off *AC-841 (+6.0 km).*

Hoteles €30–60: •*Hs* **Santiago** © 608 865 895 r/Senra 11. •*Hs* **Moure** © 981 583 637 r/dos Loureiros. •*H* **Fonte S. Roque** © 981 554 447 r/do Hospitallilo 8. •*Hs* **Estrela** © 981 576 924 Plaza de San Martín Pinario 5. •*Hs* **San Martín Pinario** *x127* © 981 560 282 *www.hsanmartinpinario.com* Praza da Inmaculada. •**Pico Sacro** r/San Francisco 22 © 981 584 466. •*H*" **Montes** © 981 574 458 *www.hotelmontes.es* r/ Raíña 11. **Rúa Fonseca** Nº1 •*P* **Fonseca** © 603 259 337. Nº5 •*Hs* **Libredon** 981 576 520 & •*P* **Barbantes / Celsa** ©981 583 271 on r/ Franco 3. **Rúa Vilar** Nº8 •*H*"**Rua Vilar** © 981 519 858. Nº17 •*H*"**Airas Nunes** © 981 569 350. Nº65 •*Hs*"**Suso** © 981 586 611 *www.hostalsuso.com*. Nº76 •*Hs* **Santo Grial** © 629 515 961. •**A Nosa Casa** © 981 585 926 r/ Entremuralles 9 adj. •*Hs* **Mapoula** © 981 580 124. •*Hs* **Alameda** © 981 588 100 San Clemente 32. ❨*€60–90:* •*H* **A Casa Peregrino** © 981 573 931 c/ Azabachería. •**Entrecercas** © 981 571 151 r/Entrecercas. **Porta de Pena** Nº17 •*H* **Costa Vella** © 981 569 530 (+ Jardín) Nº5 •*P* **Casa Felisa** © 981 582 602 (+Jardín). •**MV Algalia** © 981 558 111 Praza Algalia de Arriba 5. •*H*"**Pazo De Altamira** © 981 558 542 r/ Altamira, 18. ❨*€100+* •*H*"' **San Francisco** Campillo de San Francisco © 981 581 634.•*H*"' **Hostal de los Reyes Católicos** Plaza Obradoiro © 981 582 200.

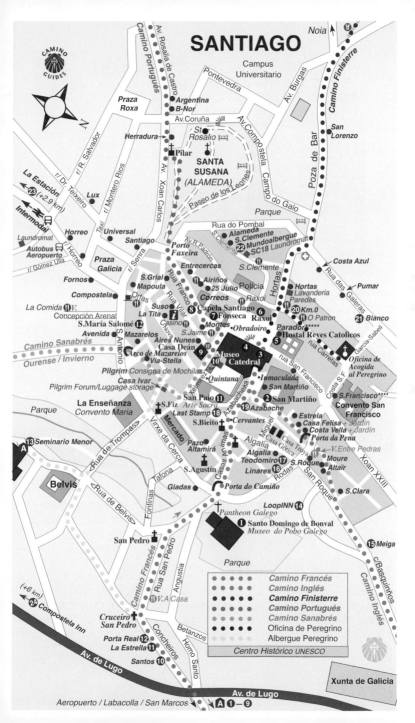

❽ The Shrine of St. James
arriving in Libredon. *Rua Franco, 5.*

The Compostela

Pilgrims Office
Rúa das Carretas

Pilgrims Chapel
Adjoining the Pilgrims Reception

Botafumeiro >

Tiraboleiros

Monumentos Históricos: ❶ Convento de Santo Domingo de Bonaval XIIIth *(panteón de Castelao, Rosalía de Castro y museo do Pobo Galego)* overlooking the Porta do Camiño where the French way enters the old city. ❷ Mosteiro de San Martín Pinario XVIth *y museo* ❸ Pazo de Xelmirez XIIth ❹ Catedral XIIth –XVIIIth *Portica de Gloria, claustro, museo e tesouro* ❺ Hostal dos Reis Católicos XVth *Parador* ❻ Pazo de Raxoi XVIIIth *Presendencia da Xunta* ❼ Colexio de Fonseca XVIth *universidade y claustro* ❽ Capela y Fonte de Santiago (where, by tradition, his body first came to rest when arriving in Libredon – now Santiago). ❾ Casa do Deán XVIIIth (original pilgrim office until its recent move to Rua das Carretas). ❿ Casa Canónica *museo Peregrinaciónes.* ⓫ Mosteiro de San Paio de Antealtares XVth *Museo de Arte Sacra.* ⓬ S.Maria Salomé XIIth.

Santiago is a wonderful destination, full of vibrancy and colour. Pilgrims, musicians, dancers, tourists... all come and add to the life and soul of this fabled city. Stay awhile and visit her museums and markets. Soak up some of her culture or relax in the delightful shaded park *Alameda* and climb to the *capela de Santa Susanna* or stroll up the avenue of the Lions *Paseo dos Leónes* to the statue of Rosalia de Castro and look out west over her belovéd Galicia and... *Finis terrae.*

PILGRIM ASSOCIATIONS:

UK: Confraternity of St. James +44 [0]2079 289 988 e-mail: *office@csj.org.uk* website: *www.csj.org.uk* pre-eminent site in English with online shop.
IRELAND: Camino Society Ireland. Based in Dublin: *www.caminosociety.ie*
U.S.A. American Pilgrims on the Camino. *www.americanpilgrims.org*
CANADA: Canadian Company of Pilgrims Canada. *www.santiago.ca*
SOUTH AFRICA: Confraternity of St. James of SA *www.csjofsa.za.org*
AUSTRALIA: Australian Friends of the Camino *www.afotc.org*

SANTIAGO:

Pilgrim Office *oficinadelperegrino.com/en*
Tourism: *www.santiagoturismo.com*
Luggage storage & transfer / forum & meeting space *www.casaivar.com*
Backpack storage & local tours *www.pilgrim.es* Rúa Nova, 7 (adj. cathedral)

INTERVIEWS WITH JOHN BRIERLEY:

The Camino Cafe Podcast: *www.leighbrennan.com*
Camino Guides: *www.caminoguides.com* under *Your Guide* and *Community*

PILGRIM WEBSITES: (in English) loosely connected with the Way of St. James or with the theme of pilgrimage that you may find helpful.

Camino Forum: Largest online camino forum *www.caminodesantiago.me*
The British Pilgrimage Trust: *www.britishpilgrimage.org*
Gatekeeper Trust *www.gatekeeper.org.uk*
Paulo Coelho reflections from author of The Pilgrimage *paulocoelhoblog.com*
Peace Pilgrim Her life and work *www.peacepilgrim.com*
The Quest A Guide to the Spiritual Journey *www.thequest.org.uk*

ALBERGUE, HOSTAL AND HOTEL BOOKING SITES:

List of albergues open in Winter: *www.aprinca.com/alberguesinvierno/*
Christian Hospitality Network: *http://en.ephatta.com*
Youth Hostels: *www.pousadasjuventude.pt/en*
Albergues: *www.onlypilgrims.com*
Hostals: *www.hostelworld.com*
Hotels, Hostals & Albergues: popular booking site *www.booking.com*
Paradores: *www.paradore.es*

PILGRIM AND BACKPACK TRANSFERS / STORES:

Spanish Postal Service: *www.elcaminoconcorreos.com/en/*
Transfers: *www.pilbeo.com/en*
Transfers and assistance: *www.pilgrim.es/en*

BIBLIOGRAPHY:

Much of the information given here comes from local information garnered along the way. Myth and legend abound and, while frequently arising from some historical occurrence they are, by their very nature, not dependent on fact. If you are interested to find additional sources of information on this route try your local library or search the internet.

• *The Bible in Spain*, by George Borrow. Originally published London, 1842
• *A Stranger in Spain*, by H.V Morton. Methuen: London, 1955.
• *Nine Faces of Christ*, by Eugene Whitworth. DeVorss 1993.
• *A Course In Miracles*, Foundation for Inner Peace. Penguin Books 1975
• *Poems – Rosalía de Castro*, translated by Anna-Marie Aldaz, Barbara N. Gantt and Anne C. Bromley. State University of New York Press, 1991.
• *A Coruna, The Port Way of Saint James: A Guide for Pilgrims*, Manuel Rodrigues, Tourism de A Coruna pamphlet.
• *The English Route,* Alicia Carrera, A Nosa Terra, Vigo
• *As Pegadas de Santiago na Cultura de Fisterra*, by Benjamin Trillo Trillo. Fundación Caixa Galicia, 1999. (Trilingual: Galego, Castellano, English)
• *O Camiño de Fisterra,* by Fernando Alonso Romero. Edicións Xerais de Galicia, 1993 (Trilingual: Galego, Castellano, English)
• *Mar Tenebroso – A costa da morte do sol,* Ramón Allegue Martínez. EuroGraficas pichel,1996. (Galego)
• *Galicia Enteira – Fisterra e Costa da Morte*, Xosé Luís Laredo Verdejo. Edicións Xerais de Galicia, 1996. (Galego)
• *El Camino del Milenio,* Ramón Allegue Martínez. Baupres Editores, 2000.
• *O Camiño dos Peregrinos á Fin do Mundo,* Antón Pombo y otros. Deputación Provincial da Coruña, 2000. (Galego)
• *The Fisterra-Muxía Way,* Manuel Rodríguez. Xunta de Galicia, 2007.

A tithe of all royalties from the sale of this book will be distributed to individuals or organisations seeking to preserve the physical and spiritual integrity of this route.

RETURNING HOME: *Some inner thoughts ...*

It is possible that after a week of walking our outer appearance might have changed, it is also possible that some inner transformation may have taken place. The time, space and pace of the camino may have allowed certain reflections and realisations to emerge about ourselves, our lives and our place in them. Stepping out of our familiar routines and systems gives us the distance to view them with fresh eyes, and in looking at our lives from afar we may gain an entirely new perspective.

What differentiates a pilgrimage from a long distance walk is that an overt purpose of pilgrimage is to bring about inner change. This change, born of awareness gained by our time on the path, may be gentle and subtle or it may hit us with a powerful force. It is possible that we will end our pilgrimage filled with gratitude for the life we have and eager to return to it. It is also possible that our familiar world will no longer support our inner change. And this realisation might engender different emotions as we come to see that choices may have to be made that could alter our previous way of life – what we do, where we work, how we pray or meditate... Indeed the purpose, focus and direction of our life may have altered.

Whatever our individual experiences, we may be in a heightened state of consciousness and sensitivity. Can we resist squeezing our itinerary and rushing back into our usual pattern of work and general lifestyle? This can be a crucial moment. How often do we witness change in ourselves and others only to see fear or lethargy come and rob us of our new understanding? This may be a good time to revisit the Self-assessment questionnaire and recall the original purpose and intention of our pilgrimage.

While change *can* happen in the twinkling of an eye, it is often experienced as a slow and painful process. So take time to integrate back into your life and be gentle with yourself. Having spent a week walking an ancient spiritual path, surrounded by the silence of nature, the pace of "normal life" may be dizzying. To give you some perspective, consider that you have just taken a week to walk a distance that can be travelled by car in a single hour.

Whatever you experience on arriving home, know that the camino will always be there, quietly waiting for you to return should you feel called to. But if you miss the pace and peace she provides you may be able to find this wherever you are, whenever you need it. We can learn to cultivate an inner state of calm in even the most dizzying of situations, we need not leave our pilgrim state of being behind. Pilgrimage is, after all, as much a state of mind as a destination.

The breeze at dawn has something to tell you. Don't go back to sleep.

Rumi

This guidebook is dedicated to awakening beyond human consciousness. It was born out of an existential crisis and the perceived need for a time to reflect on the purpose of life and its direction. Collectively devoid of inner-connectedness and a sense of the sacred, we live in a spiritual vacuum of our own making. While ensnared by our outer-directed materialistic world, we unwittingly hold the key to the door of our self-made prison. We can walk free any time we choose. We have been so long separated from our divine origins that we have forgotten what freedom feels like. In our fear of the unknown we choose to limit the potential of each new day to the familiarity of our prison surroundings. Perhaps *El Camino* will reveal the key to your own inner awakening.

As you take a well deserved rest at the end of the long road to the end of the way the question might well arise, 'Is the journey over or just beginning?' Whatever answer you receive will doubtless be right for you at this time. I wish you well in your journey Home and as I extend my humble blessings to a fellow pilgrim on the path I leave you with the words of *J R R Tolkein* from The Lord of the Rings:

> *The Road goes ever on and on*
> *Down from the door where it began.*
> *Now far ahead the Road has gone,*
> *And I must follow, if I can,*
> *Pursuing it with wary feet,*
> *Until it joins some larger way,*
> *Where many paths and errands meet.*
> *And whither then? I cannot say.*

12 Caminos de Santiago

❶ Camino Francés* 778 km
    St. Jean – Santiago
Camino Invierno*
Ponferrada – Santiago **275** km

❷ Chemin de **Paris 1000** km
    Paris – St. Jean via Tours

❸ Chemin de **Vézelay 900** km
    Vezélay – St. Jean via Bazas

❹ Chemin du **Puy 740** km
    Le Puy-en-Velay – St. Jean
    Ext. to Geneva, Budapest

❺ Chemin d'**Arles 750** km
    Arles – Somport Pass
Camino Aragonés **160** km
    Somport Pass – Óbanos
Camí San Jaume **600** km
    Port de Selva – Jaca
Camino del Piamonte **515** km
    Narbonne - Lourdes - St. Jean

❻ Camino de Madrid 320 km
    Madrid – Sahagún

Camino de **Levante 900** km
    Valencia – Zamora
    Alt. via Cuenca – Burgos

❼ Camino Mozárabe 390 km
    Granada – Mérida
    (Málaga alt. via Baena)

❽ Via de la **Plata 1,000** km
    Seville – Santiago
Camino Sanabrés Ourense **110** km

❾ Camino Portugués *Central** **640** km
    Lisboa – Porto 389 km
    Porto – Santiago 251 km
Camino Portugués *Costa** **320** km
    Porto – Santiago
    via Caminha & **Variante Espiritual***

❿ Camino Finisterre* 86 km
    Santiago – Finisterre
    via – Muxía – Santiago **114** km

⓫ Camino Inglés* 120 km
    Ferrol & Coruna – Santiago

⓬ Camino del **Norte 830** km
    Irún – Santiago via Gijón
Camino Primitivo 320 km
    Oviedo – Lugo – Melide